5 STEPS TO A >5™

500
AP Environmental Science
Questions
to know by test day

Also in the 5 Steps Series:

5 Steps to a 5: AP Environmental Science 2021

Also in the 500 AP Questions to Know by Test Day series:

5 Steps to a 5: 500 AP Biology Questions to Know by Test Day, Third Edition
5 Steps to a 5: 500 AP Calculus AB/BC Questions to Know by Test Day, Third Edition
5 Steps to a 5: 500 AP Chemistry Questions to Know by Test Day, Third Edition
5 Steps to a 5: 500 AP English Language Questions to Know by Test Day, Third Edition
5 Steps to a 5: 500 AP English Literature Questions to Know by Test Day, Third Edition
5 Steps to a 5: 500 AP European History Questions to Know by Test Day, Third Edition
5 Steps to a 5: 500 AP Human Geography Questions to Know by Test Day, Third Edition
5 Steps to a 5: 500 AP Macroeconomics Questions to Know by Test Day, Third Edition
5 Steps to a 5: 500 AP Microeconomics Questions to Know by Test Day, Third Edition
5 Steps to a 5: 500 AP Physics 1 Questions to Know by Test Day, Third Edition
5 Steps to a 5: 500 AP Physics C Questions to Know by Test Day
5 Steps to a 5: 500 AP Psychology Questions to Know by Test Day, Third Edition
5 Steps to a 5: 500 AP Statistics Questions to Know by Test Day, Third Edition
5 Steps to a 5: 500 AP U.S. Government & Politics Questions to Know by Test Day, Second Edition
5 Steps to a 5: 500 AP U.S. History Questions to Know by Test Day, Third Edition
5 Steps to a 5: 500 AP World History Questions to Know by Test Day, Third Edition

5 STEPS TO A 5

500

AP Environmental Science Questions

to know by test day

THIRD EDITION

Anaxos, Inc.

New York   Chicago   San Francisco   Athens   London   Madrid
Mexico City   Milan   New Delhi   Singapore   Sydney   Toronto

Anaxos, Inc. (Austin, TX) has been creating education and reference materials for over fifteen years. Based in Austin, Texas, the company uses writers from across the globe who offer expertise on an array of subjects just as expansive.

1 2 3 4 5 6 7 8 9   LCR   26 25 24 23 22 21

ISBN   978-1-260-47478-7
MHID   1-260-47478-X

e-ISBN   978-1-260-47479-4
e-MHID   1-260-47479-8

McGraw Hill products are available at special quantity discounts to use as premiums and sales promotions or for use in corporate training programs. To contact a representative, please visit the Contact Us pages at www.mhprofessional.com.

CONTENTS

INTRODUCTION

Congratulations! You've taken a big step toward AP success by purchasing *5 Steps to a 5: 500 AP Environmental Science Questions to Know by Test Day.* We are here to help you take the next step and score high on your AP exam so you can earn college credits and get into the college or university of your choice.

This book gives you 500 AP-style questions in both the multiple-choice and free-response formats. The questions cover all the most essential AP course material and each question includes an answer with a detailed explanation. These questions will give you valuable independent practice to supplement your regular textbook and the groundwork you are already doing in your AP classroom. This and the other books in this series are written by expert AP teachers who know your exam inside out and can familiarize you with the exam format, as well as questions that are most likely to appear on the exam.

You might be the kind of student who takes several AP courses and needs to study extra questions a few weeks before the exam for a final review. Or you might be the kind of student who puts off preparing until the last weeks before the exam. No matter what your preparation style is, you will surely benefit from reviewing these 500 questions, which closely parallel the content, format, and degree of difficulty of the questions on the actual AP exam. These questions and their answer explanations are the ideal last-minute study tool for those final few weeks before the test.

Remember the old saying "Practice makes perfect." If you practice with all the questions and answers in this book, we are certain you will build the skills and confidence needed to do great on the exam. Good luck!

—Editors of McGraw-Hill Education

Diagnostic Quiz

GETTING STARTED: THE DIAGNOSTIC QUIZ

The following questions refer to different units in this book. These questions will help you test your understanding of the concepts tested on the AP exam by giving you an idea of where you need to focus your attention as you prepare. For each question, simply circle the letter of your choice. Once you are done with the exam, check your work against the given answers, which also indicate where you can find the corresponding material in the book.

Good luck!

DIAGNOSTIC QUIZ QUESTIONS

1. The hydrologic, or water, cycle can take many different paths in the transfer of water.

    (A) Describe three different paths a drop of water can take starting from a rain cloud. Describe each path using terms such as *infiltration, evaporation,* and *transpiration.*

    (B) Discuss one of these paths using terms such as *influent, effluent, perennial,* or *ephemeral* in a specific example (e.g., a stream coming from the mountains).

    (C) The city of Springfield, Oregon, gets the majority of its water supply from groundwater. Explain what happens when too much of this water is extracted for use by the population.

      (i) Describe potential effects on nearby plants and animals.

      (ii) Describe how removing water can actually lead to flooding.

      (iii) Describe what changes can happen to the city itself from groundwater overdraft.

2. Lichens are composed of two different species, a fungus and a photosynthetic microorganism—either a cyanobacterium or an alga, and sometimes both. Together they slowly grow on a surface as a plantlike mass that appears to be a single organism. They can grow in some of the most inhospitable conditions on earth, such as high elevations, deserts, bare rock, and frozen ground. The fungus provides protection from the elements and reduces water loss by covering the whole structure in tough filaments. Sometimes the fungus slowly dissolves the substrate that its lichen is growing upon and distributes minerals throughout the lichen. All lichen fungi help to gather water, and they help to gather minerals from dust and rain. Meanwhile, the photosynthetic microorganism converts carbon dioxide in the air to carbohydrates for food that it shares with the fungus. Neither the fungus, alga, nor cyanobacterium seems to be harmed by this relationship, and none of these species can live in similar conditions alone. Some animals eat lichens, including reindeer and some humans—in Northern Europe and Asia, some people still eat a lichen called *Iceland moss*.

(A) What is the best name for the lichen relationship between a fungus and a cyanobacterium?

(B) What ecological succession role do lichens play in areas that have only bare rock?

(C) What is the relationship that a reindeer has with a lichen that it eats?

3. The silversword alliance is the name of a set of about 30 related species of plants endemic to Hawaii. Members of the sunflower family, the silversword alliance plants are all very closely related, having the same number of chromosomes and nearly the same genes. They probably developed from a single ancestor seed that came to the islands from North America about 5.2 million years ago. These species often feature long, thin leaves, sometimes with a green-silver color that gives them their collective name. But they show an astonishing morphological variety, from the small, bush-size *Argyroxiphium sandwicense* to the tall, palm tree–like *Wilkesia gymnoxiphium*. The tall, branching tree *Dubautia latifolia* lives only in the forests of the island of Kauai, while *Argyroxiphium sandwicense* recently lived only on steep cliffs on the island of Hawaii, although it once populated much of the upper portion of volcano Mauna Kea until herbivorous mammals came to the island. Recent efforts have repopulated some of the gravelly, nearly lifeless volcanic soil of Mauna Kea with *Argyroxiphium sandwicense*.

(A) Why does the silversword alliance lack genetic diversity despite the morphological diversity among its species?

(B) What is the connection between the silversword alliance's evolutionary divergence and its members' current habitats?

(C) Which of the above species is likely involved in primary succession, and why?

(D) Why did *Argyroxiphium sandwicense* probably not have some form of protection from herbivorous mammals?

4. The great-tailed grackle began to breed in Central Texas as late as the 1910s. A yellow-eyed relative of the crow measuring about 40 centimeters from the tip of its tail to the end of its long, thin beak, the great-tailed grackle settled the area after large towns and cities began to develop, and people cleared thick brush and forest for agriculture and widely spaced shade trees. Great-tailed males are black and iridescent blue, while females are smaller brown and yellow birds. Their relative, the 28-centimeter common grackle, once dominated Central Texas but is now only a visitor, even though both species have similar omnivorous diets, eating insects, small fish, berries, and unattended human food. Another related species, the boat-tailed grackle, still has essentially the same habitat as it had before large-scale human settlements came to Texas—it still lives along the Gulf of Mexico coast, overlapping with great-tailed territory in many places, although the boat-tailed bird dominates these areas.

(A) What is the likely reason that the common grackle left Central Texas when the great-tailed grackle moved in?

(B) In areas where the great-tailed and boat-tailed grackles both live, what is the boat-tailed grackle's realized niche?

(C) After the arrival of the great-tailed grackle, how does the boat-tailed grackle keep living in the same areas, while the common grackle did not?

5. Starting in the 1990s, the U.S. wild pig population exploded. Escaped domestic pigs and wild boars interbred, and their populations grew exponentially, so that by 2008, the U.S. Department of Agriculture estimated that nearly four million of the animals ran wild in more than 30 states, with the largest populations in Texas, Florida, and California. They are highly adaptable to many habitats and have a high reproductive rate, with females becoming fertile at about eight months of age and producing two litters every year, each with about six small piglets. Although sows carefully protect their brood, juveniles have a very high mortality rate, while adults have a lower mortality rate after one year. Adult wild pigs grow to more than 45 kg—about 100 pounds—and live an average of five years. True omnivores, wild pigs eat fruit, seeds, nuts, grubs, small animals, and occasionally smaller pigs. They destroy crops and are dangerous to humans, so states including Missouri have eased regulations to encourage hunters to shoot wild pigs. Other carnivores of wild pigs include wolves, bears, coyotes, birds of prey, bobcats, and cougars.

(A) Do wild pigs conform more to the characteristics of r-selected or K-selected species? In what ways do they differ from the standard for that type of species?

(B) What sort of survivorship curve best describes the mortality of wild pigs throughout their lives?

(C) During the 1990s, had wild pigs approached their environment's carrying capacity?

(D) What elements in the paragraph above comprise the environmental resistance that helps to establish wild pig carrying capacity?

6. According to the U.S. Census Bureau, between 2004 and 2005, the U.S. Northeast had 362,000 immigrants from elsewhere in the United States, while 774,000 people emigrated. An additional 323,000 people immigrated into the Northeast from other countries. During the same period, the U.S. West had 718,000 immigrants from inside the country and 655,000 people emigrating, and 597,000 people immigrated to the West from other countries. In 2004, there were about 148.9 million women in the United States and a total of 293 million people. About 61.6 million U.S. women were of reproductive age in 2004, as defined by the Census Bureau—that is, they were 15 to 44 years old. About 3.7 million of these women had given birth in the previous year.

   (A) What is the net 2003–2004 population change in the U.S. Northeast from all immigration and emigration?

   (B) Considering the U.S. Northeast and West, which region had greater overall immigration? Which had greater overall emigration?

   (C) What was the fertility of U.S. women between 2003 and 2004?

   (D) What was the fecundity of U.S. women between 2003 and 2004?

7. Physical and chemical weathering play a significant role in the rock cycle and in the formation of sedimentary rocks.

   (A) Describe three methods of physical weathering and three methods of chemical weathering that can change a rock at or near earth's surface.

   (B) After a rock has been weathered and becomes sediment, describe how it might become a sedimentary rock.

   (C) How does sediment change as it moves through the rock cycle?

8. The Pacific Ring of Fire is the name of a tectonically active area around the border of almost the entire Pacific Ocean. The volcanoes in the Ring of Fire result from the Pacific plate's movement toward or away from several different continental plates, including the North American plate, the Indo-Australian plate, and the Antarctic plate. Japan's calamitous March 2011 earthquake and tsunami were results of tectonic activity along nearby portions of the Ring of Fire. Japan's iconic Mount Fuji—the country's highest volcano—is also a product of the ring. Japan lies on a complex intersection of the Pacific plate, the Philippine plate, the Eurasian plate, and the North American plate. Japan and other islands in the area form a line that tends to follow local plate boundaries, and the region is very rich in volcanoes.

   (A) What causes the Pacific plate to move?
   (B) What process generates magma circulation?
   (C) In which direction is the Pacific plate probably moving?
   (D) The Nazca plate lies under the Pacific Ocean between the Pacific plate and the South American plate. Between the Nazca plate and the Pacific plate lie a series of ocean ridges that form a jagged line, rather than a straight line, on the ocean floor. What is this called, and what lies at each offset part of the ridge?

9. Farmer Jill started growing organic vegetables in her backyard and was so successful that she decided to purchase land and fulfill her dream of owning her own organic farm. While looking at properties, she found three properties for sale. The first is currently run as a large industrial farm but is not organic. The second is a small farm that used resource-based methods of agriculture. The third piece of land is not yet farmed.

   (A) Assume she chooses the first property. Describe two problems she would have with changing this land to an organic farm.
   (B) Describe what features she would see at the second property that directly relate to using the resource-based methods.
   (C) Assume she purchases the third property. Identify and describe
       (i) organic methods or concepts that would be used in designing and building the new organic farm
       (ii) the drawbacks of owning an organic farm
       (iii) the principles and methods of integrated pest management that would be used on the organic farm

10. Forests are disappearing from the world at a fast rate that can be remedied only by better forest management.

(A) Describe the four different methods of tree harvesting: clear-cutting, strip cutting, selective cutting, and shelterwood cutting.
  (i) Explain the process of each method of harvesting.
  (ii) Describe the environmental drawbacks of each.
  (iii) Describe the benefits of each.

(B) Describe two methods of maintaining sustainable forestry.

(C) Discuss two pieces of legislation that were passed to protect forests in the United States.

11. Around the beginning of the 21st century, fossil fuel extraction companies began to discover huge reserves of natural gas trapped in shale deposits. Recently developed improvements in hydraulic fracturing technology have allowed gas extractors to remove the fossil fuel from the ground more efficiently than was previously possible, and in 2009, the Colorado School of Mines' Potential Gas Committee recognized a record increase in U.S. natural gas reserves—about 35% more natural gas had recently become available for extraction due to the recognition of unconventional gas from shale. However, hydraulic fracturing has a growing number of critics, who are concerned that carcinogenic and otherwise dangerous chemicals from fracturing fluid may contaminate underground water supplies, while natural gas may have already leaked into water wells in Dimock, Pennsylvania.

(A) How does hydraulic fracturing help to remove natural gas from shale deposits?

(B) Does the production of unconventional natural gas from shale contribute to global warming more or less than conventional natural gas?

(C) How would hydraulic fracturing fluids or natural gas get from shale gas wells into drinking water? How deep are water wells, compared to the depth at which fracturing fluid is injected into shale deposits?

12. Using all of the energy she can get from eating a peanut butter and jelly sandwich, a woman takes as many buckets of water to the top of a hill as she can and pours them into a barrel there. She opens a valve at the bottom of the barrel, and all the water flows down a pipe running down the hill. The pipe ends halfway to the bottom, where the water strikes the paddles of a waterwheel, which turns in response. As the wheel turns, it coils a spring. Which of the following objects contained the greatest total energy?
    (A) the water in the barrel at the top of the hill, before it flowed into the pipe
    (B) the coiled spring, right when all the water had flowed from the pipe
    (C) the water moving down the pipe, right when the barrel emptied
    (D) the sandwich, before the woman took her first bite

13. Which is the largest source of tropospheric ozone pollution?
    (A) combustion of fossil fuels
    (B) water vapor from power plants
    (C) landfill decomposition
    (D) CFC emissions

14. A _____ is an air pollutant that is emitted directly from a source. A _____ is not emitted directly from a source, but will form when pollutants react in the atmosphere.
    (A) ozone; smog
    (B) primary pollutant; secondary pollutant
    (C) smog; secondary pollutant
    (D) secondary pollutant, primary pollutant

(Relative) LD-50 of Common Items

Aspirin	200
Caffeine	127
Nicotine	3.4
Table salt	3,000
Windex	>5000
Bleach	192

15. Which of the common substances in the preceding chart is considered to be the most dangerous for human health?
    (A) aspirin
    (B) caffeine
    (C) nicotine
    (D) bleach

16. Which of the following activities would contribute to increased dissolved oxygen levels in aquatic environments?
    (A) photosynthesis
    (B) respiration
    (C) decomposition
    (D) eutrophication

17. Global warming is a complex phenomenon that is influenced by many variables, including solar radiation, volcanic eruptions, human contributions to greenhouse gases, and weather system changes. The extent to which this warming occurs depends on how these variables interact with each other.
    (A) Explain how each of the variables above can affect global warming.
    (B) Give an example of a negative feedback cycle that occurs with one or more of these variables.
    (C) Give an example of a positive feedback cycle that occurs with one or more of these variables.

18. Some people are not concerned about global warming because they are unaware of the direct impact it would have on them, their children, and their grandchildren. Suppose you have family members in different areas of our nation: Uncle Joe in the Midwest, Aunt Susanna in coastal Louisiana, and Grandma Betty in New Jersey. Write one letter to all of your family members explaining the potential changes they could expect to see in their lifetime due to global warming and, in particular, explaining how each of the three relatives mentioned might be affected.

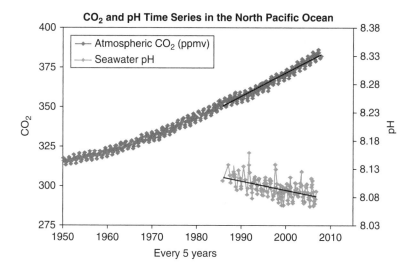

19. According to the graph, what is happening to the ocean water's pH levels as a function of carbon dioxide (CO_2) increases in the atmosphere?

   (A) As atmospheric CO_2 levels increase, the pH of ocean water increases.

   (B) As atmospheric CO_2 levels increase, the pH of ocean water decreases.

   (C) As atmospheric CO_2 levels increase, the CO_2 of the ocean water decreases.

   (D) As atmospheric CO_2 levels decrease, the CO_2 of the ocean water increases.

20. Sanitary landfills in the United States are required to use composite liners. They protect groundwater and underlying soil from any liquid that passes through the waste. This liquid can be hazardous to groundwater and soil because it has extracted dissolved and suspended matter from it as it has passed through the landfill. What is the name of this liquid?

(A) sewage
(B) landfill backwater
(C) leachate
(D) liner liquid

DIAGNOSTIC QUIZ ANSWERS

1. (Chapter 1: Living World: Ecosystems)

ANSWER: (A) One path a drop of water can take is from a rain cloud to falling as precipitation; that rain could then run off the surface of the land to the ocean. The drop would then evaporate from the ocean and eventually form clouds again.

Another path a drop of water could follow is from a rain cloud to falling as precipitation; that rain would then infiltrate the groundwater. The soil would absorb the groundwater. Plants would then take up the groundwater. The water would then transpire from parts of the plant, enter the atmosphere as water vapor, and form clouds.

A third path that a drop of water could take is from rain clouds to rain falling on a lake, with the water then evaporating from the lake and eventually forming clouds.

(B) A stream flows from the mountain and supports fish populations all year. This is known as a *perennial reach* of the stream. Farther on down the mountain, the stream may become ephemeral because it flows in those areas only in response to rainfall.

(C) (i) When too much water is taken out for use by the population, the water table drops. When this happens, trees near the river die, and animal populations die out or migrate because of loss of habitat.

(ii) When trees die off, the banks of a river are much more prone to erosion, and the river shifts its direction, causing damage to man-made structures such as roads. Water floods areas and structures that it was not intended for the river to cross.

(iii) Other changes in the city could include damage to buildings, sinkholes in roads, and settling of the land.

2. (Chapter 1: Living World: Ecosystems)

ANSWER: (A) *Mutualism* is the best name for such a relationship because both partners gain and neither appears to suffer as a result of the association.

(B) In areas with only bare rock—or in fact in any area that lacks other living things—lichens are pioneer species. They slowly adapt an area to conditions that other species find habitable. For example, some lichens living on bare rock will slowly dissolve the rock into soil.

(C) A reindeer eating lichen has a parasitic relationship with the lichen—the lichen gains nothing and loses a lot, while the reindeer gains without any known negative consequences.

3. (Chapter 2: Living World: Biodiversity)

ANSWER: (A) The silversword alliance is an excellent example of the founder effect, which is a variation of the bottleneck effect. Each species in this set is descended from a common ancestor that arrived in Hawaii very recently, in geological time. Each species has had time to acquire only minor genetic differences from that first ancestor and still shares most of the same genes in nearly the same form as they arrived in the Hawaiian archipelago.

(B) Early silversword alliance ancestors began to colonize larger areas of the Hawaiian archipelago, and those that managed to occupy a new niche, such as in the low-nutrient soil of Mauna Kea, often experienced less competition than their relatives living in more crowded niches. Gradually these plants became specialist species as their traits evolved to better fit the new niches.

(C) *Argyroxiphium sandwicense* is involved in primary succession because it inhabits nearly lifeless areas covered by volcanic rock.

(D) Because the Hawaiian Islands are difficult to reach, the herbivorous mammals were almost certainly brought by people coming to the island recently, so the plant has not had to deal with this kind of pressure on its population until recently. It takes a longer time than a few hundred years for protective genetic adaptations, such as thorns, to evolve.

4. (Chapter 2: Living World: Biodiversity)

ANSWER: (A) The common grackle probably left Central Texas due to habitat loss. The introduction of wider spaces and different vegetation favored the great-tailed grackle, and the great-tailed bird's larger size probably gave it a competitive advantage over its smaller cousin.

(B) The boat-tailed grackle's realized niche is every part of its coastal wetland niche in which it does not compete with the great-tailed grackle or other species for space, food, shelter, water, and other necessities. The boat-tailed grackle's fundamental niche includes these areas, as well as those in which it competes with the great-tailed bird.

(C) The boat-tailed grackle is likely more specialized to living along coastal areas than the great-tailed grackle, and it probably experiences less competition from the great-tailed cousin than the common grackle did, once great-tails moved in.

5. (Chapter 3: Populations)

ANSWER: (A) Wild pigs conform more to the characteristics of r-selected species. They produce many small offspring very quickly and have an early reproductive age—and thus have a high population growth rate. They often die before reaching reproductive age and are highly adaptable generalists. However, wild pigs don't have all the characteristics of r-selected species—for example, they show parental care for their offspring, and they grow to become large adults.

(B) The early loss survivorship curve best describes the mortality of wild pigs. After the pigs mature to adulthood, they tend to survive.

(C) No. Wild pig populations were still growing exponentially well into the 2000s. Approaching the environmental carrying capacity results in a population decrease soon afterward.

(D) The predators and hunters mentioned in the paragraph comprise environmental resistance to the wild pig population.

6. (Chapter 3: Populations)

ANSWER: (A) During that period, the U.S. Northeast had a net emigration of 89,000 people. That is, the population shrank by 89,000 people.

(B) The West had greater immigration by 630,000 people. That is, 630,000 more people moved to the West than to the Northeast between 2003 and 2004. The Northeast had greater emigration than the West, by 119,000 people.

(C) The fertility rate of women during this period was 3.7 million births per 148.9 million women, or about 2.5%.

(D) The fecundity rate during this period among women was at least 61.6 million births per 148.9 million women, or at least 41.4%.

7. (Chapter 4: Earth Systems and Resources)

ANSWER: (A) Physical weathering processes include frost wedging (water infiltrating a crack in a rock, expanding as it freezes, and enlarging the crack), salt wedging (salt crystals forming as water evaporates, expanding, and putting pressure on a rock), and unloading (rocks that have been buried under pressure coming to the surface, expanding, and cracking). Chemical weathering processes include oxidation (the reaction of a substance with oxygen), hydrolysis (the reaction of a substance with water), and acid precipitation (the reaction of a substance with acidic rain or snow).

(B) Weathered sediment can become sedimentary rock as it is carried by gravity, air, or water and settles in a process called deposition. Over time, buried sediment is compacted. Often natural cement, such as calcium carbonate, hematite, or quartz, acts to further bind the particles together into a sedimentary rock such as sandstone.

(C) Sediment can be compacted or cemented to form sedimentary rock. Sedimentary rock can be weathered back into loose sediments again, or it can go on to become igneous or metamorphic rock through the rock cycle. Sedimentary rock that melts into magma hardens into an igneous rock as it cools. Sedimentary rock that is subjected to heat or pressure can turn into a metamorphic rock.

8. (Chapter 4: Earth Systems and Resources)

ANSWER: (A) Convection currents in the earth's mantle cause the overlying tectonic places to move.

(B) Magma circulates as part of a process called *convection*, in which heat causes deeper magma to expand and rise. As it does this, it cools and begins to fall. The heat is generated by tidal forces on the earth's interior and by the decay of radioactive elements it contains.

(C) The Pacific plate is generally moving in a northwest direction.

(D) These are fracture zones, and at each point where the ocean ridge is offset, there is a transform fracture that is usually perpendicular to the ridge.

9. (Chapter 5: Land and Water Use)

ANSWER: (A) There are several problems Farmer Jill could have with choosing the first property. Two of these problems include ridding the land of pesticides and herbicides that are already in the soil and converting mechanized irrigation to drip irrigation. Additional problems include replenishing the soil, which would be lacking in nutrients from use of industrial fertilizers and overuse, and rehabilitating the soil structure that would be damaged from tilling.

(B) The second property would have used contour plowing methods. It would have drip irrigation, and the soil would not have been tilled. The previous farmer would use natural enemies of pests such as ladybugs and lacewings. The use of pesticides would be limited.

(C) (i) Creating the new organic farm would mean using no pesticides, using no artificial fertilizers, and no tilling of soil. Drip irrigation and alternating and interplanting crops would also be important.

(ii) Despite the many benefits, the drawbacks of owning an organic farm include cost of organic certification, cost of organic chemicals, reduced yields due to rotating or resting the soil, and the loss of crops due to insects and weeds.

(iii) The principles of integrated pest management include control but not eradication of pests, the use of natural agents, and the concept of managing an ecosystem instead of dealing with each species separately. The methods of integrated pest management include use of only natural, Organic Materials Review Institute (OMRI)–certified chemicals, more types of crops planted together, use of natural enemies of pests (ladybugs, lacewings, décolleté snails), no-till agriculture, and development of genetically resistant plants.

10. (Chapter 5: Land and Water Use)

ANSWER: (A) (i) Clear-cutting involves removing all trees in a large designated area and then burning whatever is left. Strip cutting involves clear-cuts in smaller areas in thin strips that reseed themselves. Selective cutting involves selecting out certain species from a diverse forest and cutting the mature trees, leaving the smaller trees intact. Shelterwood cutting involves removing the lesser-quality trees first, leaving the healthier trees standing. A few trees get harvested, and then the rest of the mature trees get harvested after all the seedlings have matured.

(ii) The drawbacks of clear-cuts involve increasing runoff, decreasing nutrients in food left for other species, unpleasant appearance of clear-cut areas, soil erosion, fragmentation of wildlife habitat, and loss of species. For strip cutting, the drawbacks are few but may include loss of revenue due to limited areas that can be cut. In the case of selective cutting, it takes more time to harvest fewer trees, and it also removes the best trees, so the forest does not get reseeded with the best trees. In addition, the use of roads and heavy equipment can damage the forest. For shelterwood cutting, the biggest drawback is that it costs the most.

(iii) The benefits of clear-cutting are that nutrients get cycled from burning, and it is cost-efficient. For strip cutting, the benefits include reduced erosion and less impact on the aesthetics of the environment. In selective cutting, the forest appearance is preserved, as is the variety of species. In shelterwood cutting, the aesthetics and habitat are preserved, and erosion is minimized.

(B) Sustainable forestry ensures that the forests provide necessary timber while protecting the forest enough to guarantee that it will be able to provide timber in the future. The forest can be protected this way by (1) using fewer timber products; (2) managing the forest in a holistic manner that accounts for all of the components of the ecosystem, not just the trees; (3) setting aside forestland as a preserve; and (4) replanting trees.

(C) One piece of legislation that protects forests in the United States is the Wilderness Act of 1964, which designates wilderness areas and makes rules about people's activities in those areas. Another piece of legislation is the Federal Land Policy and Management Act of 1976, which sets aside wilderness areas in government-owned areas of forest.

11. (Chapter 6: Energy Resources and Consumption)

ANSWER: (A) Hydraulic fracturing involves forcing high-pressure fluid—a liquid or gas—into the rock at the bottom of a well. This fluid forces the nearby rock to crack, releasing pockets of trapped natural gas that can be removed through the well.

(B) The production of natural gas by hydraulic fracturing releases much more methane into the atmosphere than the production of conventional natural gas. The two gases produce the same amount of carbon dioxide when burned, however.

(C) At an average of 5 to 250 meters deep, water wells are typically not nearly as deep as wells for producing natural gas from shale, which are usually 1,500 to 6,500 meters deep. So hydraulic fracturing fluid or gas must flow through a great deal of rock to get into water supplies, and it may do so through existing crevices and pores, but the flow of fluids through deep underground rock is not well understood.

12. (Chapter 6: Energy Resources and Consumption)

ANSWER: (D) Each step in the process involves some loss of energy as heat, including the coiling of the spring and the flowing of the water down the pipe. Only the sandwich originally stored all the energy transferred in this scenario.

13. (Chapter 7: Atmospheric Pollution)

ANSWER: (A) The most significant source of tropospheric ozone is from emissions from the combustion of fossil fuels. Tropospheric ozone levels have increased dramatically since the Industrial Revolution.

14. (Chapter 7: Atmospheric Pollution)

ANSWER: (B) Primary pollutants are air pollutants that are emitted directly from a source (such as a power plant). Secondary pollutants require a chemical reaction between two or more primary pollutants to form.

15. (Chapter 8: Aquatic and Terrestrial Pollution)

ANSWER: (C) Nicotine has the lowest LD-50, so a smaller dose would be needed to be a lethal dose to 50% of the population. When you are looking at the LD-50 value of a substance, smaller numbers are the most toxic.

16. (Chapter 8: Aquatic and Terrestrial Pollution)

ANSWER: (A) Photosynthesis would increase oxygen rates in aquatic environments. All of the others would increase oxygen demand, lowering dissolved oxygen levels in an aquatic system.

17. (Chapter 9: Global Change)

ANSWER: (A) The amount of energy coming from the sun changes over time, with the warmer periods on earth correlating to times in which more energy was being radiated from the sun, and the Ice Ages correlating to times when there was less solar radiation. Although there is a correlation, the effect is small compared to that of greenhouse gases, especially those generated by human activities. Volcanoes contribute to global cooling temporarily because the volcanic ash interferes with solar radiation. Greenhouse gases such as carbon dioxide absorb solar radiation that is being emitted toward space, increasing the temperatures here on earth. Weather system changes such as El Niño occur approximately every five years and last just over a year. Their occurrence is expected to be more frequent as the earth warms. They cause the ocean to become a heat source, temporarily increasing temperatures in the atmosphere.

    (B) Negative feedback will help keep global warming in check. An example of negative feedback in global warming is when the warmer air caused by global warming then creates more precipitation in northern latitudes. This can increase the amount of snow and ice in the area, which will reflect more of the incoming energy from the sun back to space, leading to cooling.

    (C) Positive feedback will make global warming an even bigger problem. An example of positive feedback would be that warming temperatures would cause snow and glaciers to melt, which means less energy is reflected back into space and is instead absorbed by the atmosphere, leading to even higher temperatures.

18. (Chapter 9: Global Change)

ANSWER:

> Dear family,
> I know there has been a lot of controversy surrounding global warming. There are a variety of opinions and possible scenarios that we might see in the future. I am writing to you out of concern for the well-being of each family member. Uncle Joe, I know you are already struggling to make money on your farm there in Iowa. Well, we will probably expect to see more droughts, hotter summers that will lessen the corn harvest, and more competition from farmland

that becomes available in Canada. Aunt Susanna, I am concerned for your safety after the last flood. I know you cannot get your house insured now for flooding, and now that you are getting older, I wonder how you will evacuate and rebuild in the event of the next hurricane. Grandma Betty, we need to make some changes after a few of your neighbors were hospitalized for West Nile virus last summer. We need to write to your local legislators and insist that government intervention is stepped up in mosquito control and eradication. We also need to insist on a cap of greenhouse gas emissions for the state of New Jersey, as well as higher mileage requirements for cars. Since you are getting older, West Nile virus is more of a threat to you than to younger people. There is a bill coming up for a vote in Congress this week on reducing greenhouse gas emissions. Please contact your local senator to support this vote because it will help reduce the problems I listed above. Thanks.
Love, Sam

19. (Chapter 9: Global Change)

ANSWER: (B) As CO_2 increases in the atmosphere, CO_2 is also dissolved in the ocean water through diffusion, wind, and wave action. This dissolved CO_2 causes a decrease in pH levels in the ocean over time. This process is called ocean acidification.

20. (Chapter 9: Global Change)

ANSWER: (C) "Leachate" is the term used to describe the water that has been filtered through the landfill and is later collected. The water is usually used to re-compact the landfill daily and then later collected at the bottom of the landfill. Eventually, the leachate is pumped out and sent to a treatment facility to be used locally.

CHAPTER 1

Living World: Ecosystems

21. In the limestone caves of Illinois, food comes from only a few sources. Heavy rains wash plants and other organic debris into the caves occasionally, but most of the food comes from outside by way of animals. Sometimes animals die deep in these caves, but much of the underground ecosystem depends on their droppings. Raccoon, frogs, cave crickets, and especially bats forage outside for food and leave fecal matter on cave floors. Bacteria and fungi break down these droppings into their mineral constituents and are themselves eaten by animals, such as millipedes and flatworms. Spiders, salamanders, and other animals catch and eat these animals when possible, but most cave dwellers can survive for a very long time without any food at all.

    (A) What producers does this cave ecosystem depend upon?
    (B) Which of these species are the cave equivalent of primary consumers?
    (C) Which of these species are the secondary consumers?

22. A temperate rain forest, such as the one on the west coast of North America, primarily has

    (A) conifer trees, wet climate, mild temperatures
    (B) flat-leaf trees, wet climate, hot temperatures
    (C) conifer trees, dry climate, mild temperatures
    (D) flat-leaf trees, wet climate, mild temperatures

23. The role that organisms play in an ecosystem is known as a(n)

    (A) old-growth forest
    (B) landscape
    (C) niche
    (D) community forest

24. Ecosystems typically include all of the following EXCEPT

    (A) decomposers
    (B) producers
    (C) abiotic chemicals
    (D) speculators

25. Plants use nitrogen to make

    (A) proteins
    (B) sugar
    (C) CO_2
    (D) O_2

26. Which of the following types of organisms are usually the first to suffer when an ecosystem is disrupted?

    (A) decomposers and detritus feeders
    (B) producers
    (C) primary consumers
    (D) tertiary consumers

27. All of the following help determine an animal's niche EXCEPT

    (A) its temperature-range tolerance
    (B) physical damage it has sustained
    (C) its adaptive traits
    (D) its typical territorial size

28. All of the following are major carbon storage reservoirs EXCEPT

    (A) fossil fuels
    (B) sedimentary rocks
    (C) the air
    (D) the earth's core

29. Deep in the ocean, falling calcium-carbonate shells dissolve at a certain depth, while they collect at a slightly shallower depth. The dividing line between these depths is known as
    (A) a thermocline
    (B) a lithosphere
    (C) the estuarine zone
    (D) a lysocline

30. Unless these two natural phenomena are in balance, global atmospheric carbon dioxide accumulates rapidly:
    I. respiration
    II. photosynthesis
    III. sedimentation
    IV. subduction
    (A) I and II
    (B) II and III
    (C) I and IV
    (D) III and IV

31. Nitrogen is an essential element for many biologically important molecules, but organisms can use atmospheric N_2 only once it has been altered by
    (A) biomineralization or dissolution in water
    (B) volcanic eruptions or reactions with sunlight
    (C) the decomposition of organisms or respiration
    (D) lightning or soil-bacteria processes

32. Which of the following human activities can alter both the carbon and nitrogen cycles at the same time?
    (A) allowing artificial fertilizer to run into rivers and streams
    (B) growing large numbers of livestock whose waste adds gases to these cycles
    (C) constructing dams that obstruct the natural paths of rivers
    (D) destroying existing vegetation-rich ecosystems, such as forests

33. The term *nitrification* describes which process?
    (A) the conversion of N_2 to NO
    (B) the conversion of N_2 to NH_3
    (C) the conversion of NH_3 to NO_2^- and NO_3^-
    (D) the conversion of N_2 to N_2O

34. One negative effect of human interference in the nitrogen cycle is
    (A) the production of rain containing nitric acid
    (B) a decrease in species that thrive on high levels of nitrogen compounds
    (C) increased ozone in the stratosphere
    (D) a decrease in the total amount of nitrogen present in the atmosphere

35. The term *geochemical cycle* describes
    (A) the production and breakdown of man-made synthetic materials
    (B) the movement of sulfur and other gases from the mantle into the atmosphere
    (C) the movement of elements through a repeating series of chemical forms
    (D) the movement of magma in the earth's mantle

36. Plants directly interact with the biological carbon cycle through
    I. respiration
    II. photosynthesis
    III. decomposition
    (A) only I and II
    (B) only II and III
    (C) only I and III
    (D) I, II, and III

37. Most of the carbon in the earth's crust is stored in
    (A) the atmosphere
    (B) ocean sediments and sedimentary rocks
    (C) fossil fuels
    (D) plants

38. Nitrification results in the two final products
    (A) ammonia and nitrogen gas
    (B) nitrate ions and nitrite ions
    (C) DNA and proteins
    (D) ozone gas and oxygen gas

39. Volcanoes release a great deal of gas when they erupt, but the composition of those gases depends on the magma type. A certain volcano in the Pacific Ocean releases about 49% carbon dioxide, 37% water vapor, 12% sulfur dioxide, and 1.5% carbon monoxide.
    (A) How does carbon cross over from the biological carbon cycle to this part of the geological carbon cycle?
    (B) What is the process by which sulfur dioxide from this volcano can become a component of organisms?
    (C) How does carbon make its way from volcanic carbon dioxide emissions into organisms?

40. Calcium stored in subsurface rock can return to the surface, but it usually does so as a result of
    (A) tectonic plate movement pushing these rock layers upward
    (B) erupting volcanoes spewing calcium-rich magma
    (C) chemical reactions releasing calcium-rich gas, which diffuses upward
    (D) these rock layers slowly dissolving into the oceans

41. Evaporation involves the conversion of
    (A) latent heat into solar energy
    (B) solar energy into latent heat
    (C) chemical energy into solar energy
    (D) potential energy into kinetic energy

42. Ecologists divide the open ocean into the euphotic zone, the bathyal zone, and the abyssal zone based mostly on
    (A) the creatures that live in each
    (B) the amount of sunlight that each receives
    (C) the salinity of each
    (D) the temperature of each

43. In which freshwater lake zone would you expect to find the greatest concentration of waterborne plants?
    (A) the benthic zone
    (B) the profundal zone
    (C) the limnetic zone
    (D) the littoral zone

44. If the residence time of N_2 is 400 million years, then
    (A) fusion reactions first created the N_2 400 million years ago
    (B) each molecule of N_2 remains chemically unchanged for an average of 400 million years
    (C) nitrogen's total duration as a nitrate and as a nitrite is an average of 400 million years
    (D) no molecule of N_2 lasts longer than 400 million years

45. Warm Caribbean water travels north past Canada to Northern Europe in the
    (A) Equatorial Countercurrent
    (B) Humboldt Current
    (C) Labrador Current
    (D) Gulf Stream Current

46. Of the following pairs of ecosystems, which has the highest net primary productivity?
    (A) swamps and estuaries
    (B) woodland and agricultural land
    (C) savannas and coniferous forests
    (D) open ocean and tundra

47. Which of the following trophic levels contain animals that eat herbivores?
    I.   tertiary consumers
    II. secondary consumers
    III. primary consumers
    IV. producers
    (A) I and II
    (B) II and III
    (C) III and IV
    (D) I and III

48. Most terrestrial phosphate originates from
    (A) freshwater lakes
    (B) uplifted rock
    (C) phosphate-fixing bacteria
    (D) the air

49. Humans' release of excess phosphates into lakes and rivers can result in
    (A) the poisoning of herbivores
    (B) phosphate-based gases depleting the ozone layer
    (C) acid rain
    (D) the overgrowth of aquatic bacteria and algae

50. In which of the following nutrient cycles does the key nutrient remain chemically unchanged throughout?
    (A) the sulfur cycle
    (B) the nitrogen cycle
    (C) the hydrologic cycle
    (D) the phosphorus cycle

51. Which of the following terms specifically describes the hydrologic cycle's distribution of water around the world, especially from the oceans to land?
    (A) transpiration
    (B) precipitation
    (C) evaporation
    (D) transport

52. The hydrologic cycle is driven by
    (A) the earth's rotation
    (B) magma convection in the earth's interior
    (C) heat from the sun
    (D) the moon's gravity

53. Which term describes water moving through soil and permeable rock to groundwater storage aquifers?
    (A) infiltration
    (B) percolation
    (C) condensation
    (D) transpiration

54. Of the following hydrologic events, which is most accelerated by hot, dry conditions?

(A) percolation
(B) condensation
(C) transpiration
(D) precipitation

55. Which of the following processes requires condensation nuclei in order to occur?

(A) water vapor condensing into moisture droplets in clouds
(B) liquid water evaporating from land
(C) evaporation of liquid water into water vapor
(D) purification of liquid water by decomposer bacteria

CHAPTER 2

Living World: Biodiversity

56. Compared with a population with low genetic diversity, a genetically diverse population is more likely to include individuals that

(A) are distributed over a large range
(B) vary greatly by age
(C) vary greatly by appearance and behavior
(D) each carry a large number of genes

57. Genetic diversity, species diversity, ecological diversity, and functional diversity are best characterized as elements of

(A) cultural diversity
(B) trophic levels
(C) abiotic resources
(D) biological diversity

58. When biologists speak of "survival of the fittest," which of the following attributes do they consider most important to the concept?

(A) the ability of the fastest individuals to avoid predators
(B) the ability of the strongest individuals to capture prey
(C) the ability of the most fertile individuals to successfully reproduce
(D) the ability of the most high-tolerance individuals to withstand temperature extremes

59. Which of the following best describes the term "endemic species"?
    (A) a species colonizing a far-flung new range
    (B) a species that benefits from its relationship with a second species
    (C) a species found in one specific region
    (D) a species that spreads disease

60. Conservation biologists have an emergency action plan for identifying and protecting about 25 "hot spots" because they contain
    (A) the majority of the earth's freshwater reserves
    (B) about ⅗ of the earth's mineral nutrients
    (C) about ⅔ of the earth's terrestrial biodiversity
    (D) about ⅓ of the earth's marine biodiversity

61. All of the following are elements of an organism's habitat EXCEPT its
    (A) food
    (B) water
    (C) shelter
    (D) reproductive strategy

Regulating:	Supporting:	Cultural:	Provisioning:
Climate, Air Quality, Soil erosion, Pollination	Cycles (Water, Carbon, Nitrogen), Photosynthesis	Recreation, Ecotourism, Ethics and Inspiration	Natural medicines, access to fresh water, fuel, fibers, and food

Figure 2.1

62. Ecosystem services are the important benefits to humans that arise from healthy, functioning ecosystems. Ecosystems can be essential to human mental and physical health and survival. Using Figure 2.1 as a guide, under which category would you place whitewater rafting down the Colorado River?

(A) regulating
(B) supporting
(C) cultural
(D) provisioning

63. A population of island birds has a very homogeneous genetic pool. Which of the following can result in greater genetic diversity?

(A) a small number of birds leaving to start a new colony
(B) a bottleneck event
(C) genetic drift
(D) inbreeding

64. A new island is colonized by a small number of mice that occasionally trade members with mainland mice when the receding tide reveals a land bridge between the two. This is an example of
    (A) a bottleneck event
    (B) a metapopulation
    (C) the founder effect
    (D) genetic drift

65. A species is most likely to go extinct in a changing environment if it has
    (A) high genetic diversity
    (B) a large niche
    (C) a narrow niche
    (D) recent evolutionary adaptations

66. Coastal beaches and barrier islands are eroded by
    (A) jetties
    (B) percolation
    (C) longshore currents
    (D) compaction

67. Which of the following is correct regarding island biogeography?
    (A) Smaller islands have more species richness.
    (B) The smallest islands have the fewest resources due to less habitat area.
    (C) Larger islands have less species richness due to more competition for resources.
    (D) Larger islands would have fewer resources than smaller islands.

68. According to the island biogeography equilibrium model, if you look at two islands that are the same size, but one is 10 miles away from the mainland and one is 100 miles away from the mainland, which island will have the higher immigration rate?

a. The closest island will have a higher immigration rate.

b. The furthest island will have a higher immigration rate.

c. Immigration rate will depend on the size of the island.

(A) a only

(B) b only

(C) c only

(D) a and c

69. Your environmental consulting company has been hired by the U.S. government to determine what type of islands are the most desirable to save native plants and animals that may migrate from the mainland. Which island would be best to invest your time in protecting to save the most biodiversity?

(A) islands that are near the mainland and small in size

(B) islands that are near the mainland and large in size

(C) islands that are far away from the mainland and small in size

(D) islands that are far away from the original population and larger in size

70. There are two types of main habitat niches in ecosystems. A fundamental niche represents all the environmental conditions (both abiotic and biotic) in which a species can live. The organism can occupy the niche without competition from other species or pressure from predators. When an organism has competition for food or breeding partners or if predators appear in the area, the niche will narrow. What is the term for the habitat niche an organism will hold when faced with environmental pressures, such as competition or predation?

(A) actual niche

(B) competitive advantage

(C) competitive exclusion

(D) realized niche

Use the following graph for Questions 71–74.

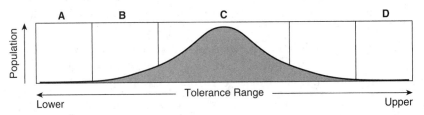

Figure 2.2

71. As shown in Figure 2.2, Jennifer has a classroom aquarium that includes goldfish, various other species of fish, and some small aquatic plants. She wants to increase the aquarium's health, so she adds some more plants to the tank. The plants provide more dissolved oxygen and places for her fish to hide. As a result, her goldfish population doubles in two months.

    Which of the following statements is supported by this scenario?

    (A) The turbidity of the tank was a limiting factor.
    (B) The dissolved oxygen levels in the tank was a limiting factor.
    (C) The size of her tank was a limiting factor.
    (D) The amount of goldfish was a limiting factor.

72. In the aquarium scenario above, what would happen to the fish if all of the plants suddenly died off and decomposition used up all of the dissolved oxygen in the tank?

    (A) A
    (B) B
    (C) C
    (D) D

73. A forest has a variety of trees and other plant species. The trees provide shade to some plant species that do not like a lot of direct sunlight. Using the preceding graph above, which section (A–D) would have a decreasing abundance of plants due to having too much direct sunlight (not enough shade coverage)?

(A) A
(B) B
(C) C
(D) D

74. In which section (A–D) would you find the highest biodiversity?

(A) A
(B) B
(C) C
(D) D

75. Ecosystems can be disrupted through natural forces such as volcanic eruptions that destroy or cover up all the topsoil that plants need to grow. When this happens, the underlying bedrock must be broken down into soil over time by organisms that are suited for that harsh, new environment. Over time, this breakdown will allow the soil to be replenished and plants to come back to the area. What are these first species that are established in a newly disturbed environment called?

(A) invasive species
(B) keystone species
(C) primary species
(D) pioneer species

76. This is the final stage or the "end-stage" of ecological succession.

(A) primary community
(B) climax community
(C) end community
(D) resting community

77. Which of the following ecological disturbances would be considered to be anthropogenic?
    (A) hurricane
    (B) coastal flooding
    (C) logging
    (D) tsunami

78. Many ecosystems have evolved with fire as an essential component of the health of that ecosystem. Many plant species in fire-affected environments require fire to germinate seeds, clear out old growth, and establish new seedlings. Which of the following biomes does not need fire as a contributor to ecosystem renewal or seed germination?
    (A) prairie
    (B) savanna
    (C) chaparral
    (D) tropical rainforests

79. A tsunami is a series of great sea waves that can cause great ecological destruction. Which of the following is LEAST likely the cause of triggering a tsunami?
    (A) earthquakes
    (B) hurricanes
    (C) volcanoes
    (D) landslides

80. Only 5% of a population of lizards survive a major flood, and by chance, the majority of survivors are green. If the original population was composed mostly of brown individuals, then which phenomenon has likely occurred?
    (A) evolutionary divergence
    (B) a bottleneck event
    (C) parallel evolution
    (D) natural selection

81. Compared to beneficial mutations, harmful mutations are
    (A) more common
    (B) equally common
    (C) nonexistent
    (D) less common

82. In which of the following situations has evolution most likely taken place?
    (A) An individual produces only taller offspring.
    (B) A population produces offspring that are representative of the gene pool.
    (C) A population recombines with an isolated group of distantly related individuals.
    (D) A population's allele frequencies have changed over time.

83. After splitting into two isolated populations, genetic changes make it impossible for an individual from one of the two populations to reproduce with an individual from the other. Which term most accurately describes what has happened?
    (A) a bottleneck event
    (B) differential reproduction
    (C) natural selection
    (D) speciation

84. A founder group of cats arrives on an isolated island and after thousands of generations produces several different cat species that each prey on different kinds and sizes of animals. This is an example of
    (A) evolutionary divergence
    (B) coevolution
    (C) commensalism
    (D) competitive exclusion

Slash and burn grasses, weeds, shrubs   Pine trees   Dense forest

Agriculture   Many species

Year 0   Year 200

Figure 2.3

85. The diagram in Figure 2.3 illustrates

   (A) primary succession
   (B) secondary succession
   (C) tertiary succession
   (D) pioneer plants

86. Succession is a biological process by which a community successively changes into another and continues on until a climax community is reached. Which type of succession is formed when an environment has been disturbed, such as when a large fire comes through, but the soil underneath is maintained and still viable to support life?

   (A) primary succession
   (B) invasive succession
   (C) secondary succession
   (D) pioneer succession

87. Lichens are a very important pioneer species that grow on bedrock and help to break it down into soil over time. They are integral in providing suitable soil for plants to be able to become re-established in a disturbed environment. Lichen is a symbiotic relationship between two organisms: which two organisms are they?

   (A) algae and fungi
   (B) algae and bacteria
   (C) fungi and bacteria
   (D) fungi and moss

88. Southeast Asian flying foxes are responsible for pollinating most durian tree flowers and spreading durian seeds. Durian fruit and durian trees support a vast array of other species, such that a decline in the flying fox population could have disastrous effects for the local ecology. As a result, flying foxes can probably be considered

(A) an indicator species

(B) an invasive species

(C) a keystone species

(D) a parasitic species

89. As a series of communities of organisms colonize a new area, trees become established

(A) early in secondary succession

(B) early in primary succession

(C) late in primary succession

(D) late in secondary succession

90. During primary succession, which of the following organisms often serve as pioneer species?

(A) lichens

(B) grasses

(C) small herbs

(D) trees

CHAPTER 3

Populations

91. Why would a panda be more sensitive to environmental changes in its habitat versus another species such as a raccoon?

(A) Raccoons live in cities and eat out of trash cans.
(B) Pandas are on the endangered species list.
(C) Pandas are specialists that have a very narrow habitat and have a specific source of food.
(D) Raccoons are limited to only berries and nuts.

92. One species benefits from its relationship with another species for whom the relationship does no harm nor good. This relationship is best described as

(A) commensalism
(B) parasitism
(C) ecological succession
(D) mutualism

93. Koalas are native to Australia. They only eat eucalyptus leaves.

Giraffes use their long necks and long, muscular tongues to remove acacia leaves from their spiky branches without injury.

Honey badgers will chase other predators away from carcasses. They can use their claws to dig burrows, find yams, and break open beehives.

The Canada lynx is best adapted to snowy, mountainous forests and hunt the snowshoe hare.

Using the information above, which of the following species would you choose as a niche generalist?

(A) koala
(B) giraffes
(C) honey badgers
(D) Canadian lynx

94. Of the following characteristics, which three are typical of K-selected species?
  I. late successional colonization
  II. early reproductive age
  III. generalist niche
  IV. small size in adulthood
  V. few but large offspring
  VI. specialist niche

(A) I, II, and III
(B) II, III, and IV
(C) II, IV, and V
(D) I, V, and VI

95. Which of the following lists of terms is organized from most specific to most inclusive?

(A) community, population, ecosystem

(B) population, community, ecosystem

(C) species, ecosystem, population

(D) individual, community, population

96. As opposed to a K-selected species, an r-selected species usually has

(A) numerous relatively small offspring

(B) offspring that tend to survive to reproductive age

(C) a population that stays close to the environment's carrying capacity

(D) high parental care of offspring

97. Depending partly on their reproductive strategies, different organisms have different life expectancies described by survivorship curves. The three general survivorship curves are

   I. constant loss

  II. erratic loss

 III. early loss

 IV. logarithmic loss

   V. late loss

(A) I, II, and V

(B) II, III, and IV

(C) I, III, and V

(D) II, III, and V

Species Survivorship Selection Characteristics

r-Selected Species	K-Selected Species
Unstable environment	Stable environment
Small-sized organisms	Large-sized organisms
Many offspring, low offspring care	Few offspring, large offspring care
Short life expectancy	Long life expectancy
Density independent	Density dependent

Figure 3.1

98. Using Figure 3.1 as a reference, determine which of the following graphs would represent a K-selected population.

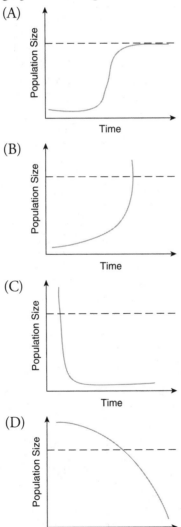

(A)

(B)

(C)

(D)

Use Figure 3.2 for Questions 99–101.

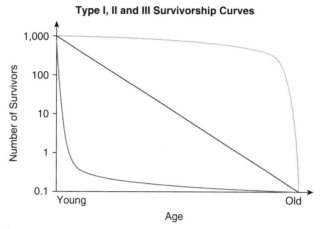

Figure 3.2

99. Songbirds that die off at a steady rate throughout their lifetime have which type of survivorship curve?
    (A) Type I
    (B) Type II
    (C) Type III
    (D) Type IV

100. Humans have which type of survivorship curve?
    (A) Type I
    (B) Type II
    (C) Type III
    (D) Type IV

101. Which of the following exhibits survivorship Type III—high death rate early in life and low survival rate during the earliest life stages?
    (A) humans
    (B) songbirds
    (C) chickens
    (D) turtles

102. Limiting factors determine the carrying capacity of an organism in an environment. Which of these is considered to be a density-independent factor of carrying capacity?

(A) competition
(B) predation
(C) disease
(D) flooding

103. Americans use up about 25% of the world's natural resources, such as trees and fossil fuels. The impact that a single person has on the environment is expressed as the amount of land that is required to sustain their lifestyle and consumption of natural resources. This is referred to as an individual's

(A) ecological footprint
(B) carrying capacity
(C) ecological impact
(D) carrying load

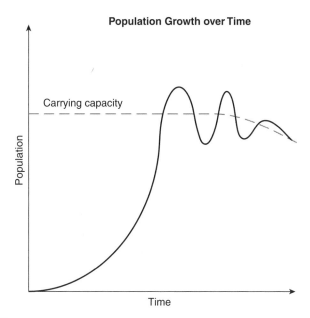

Figure 3.3

104. See Figure 3.3. _____ occurs when the population growth exceeds the carrying capacity, leading to a die-off for individuals in the population.

(A) unstable equilibrium

(B) overshoot

(C) degraded carrying capacity

(D) ecosystem collapse

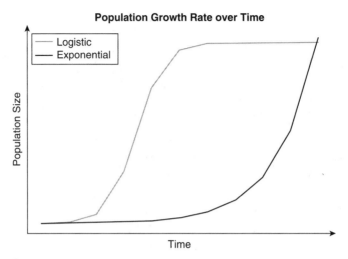

Figure 3.4

105. Based on Figure 3.4, which of these scenarios represent exponential growth?

    (A) Yeast, used to make bread and alcoholic beverages, will grow rapidly and then level off as the population depletes all of the nutrients that it needs for its growth.

    (B) With harbor seals, the population size will exceed the carrying capacity for a short period of time, and then it will fall below the carrying capacity again as the availability of food diminishes.

    (C) One thousand bacteria are placed in a petri dish with a supply of nutrients, and the number of bacteria will have doubled after just an hour. The next hour, each of the new two thousand bacteria will double again, producing four thousand bacteria. After a day, the population would have increased from one thousand to more than 16 billion bacteria.

    (D) The resources are plentiful and the growth rate is rapid when few individuals of the species are present. As the population levels off when it reaches the carrying capacity of the environment, the growth rate will slow.

106. Which of the following would cause a global impact related to human population growth?

(A) Converting forested land into agricultural fields; reduces the carbon dioxide (CO_2) uptake by plants.

(B) Converting forested land into agricultural fields can cause increased soil erosion.

(C) Converting forested land into agricultural fields can cause sediment runoff.

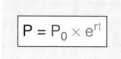

Figure 3.5

107. In the population growth formula shown in Figure 3.5, what does "r" stand for?

(A) total population after time

(B) starting population size

(C) percentage rate of growth

(D) Euler's number

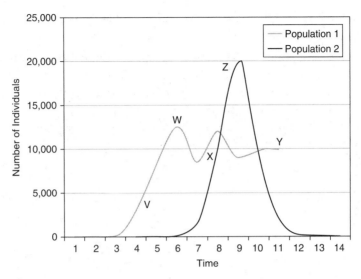

Figure 3.6

Questions 108–114 refer to the two curves plotted on the graph in Figure 3.6. They represent two different populations undergoing different patterns of change over time. Lettered points on each curve represent different moments in each group's population changes.

108. At point V, Population 1 is

(A) slowing its growth
(B) overshooting the environment's carrying capacity
(C) growing exponentially
(D) experiencing environmental resistance

109. What is the approximate carrying capacity of the environment experienced by Population 1?

(A) 8,000
(B) 10,000
(C) 13,000
(D) 15,000

110. Between points W and Y, Population 1 is experiencing

  (A) a population crash
  (B) exponential growth
  (C) geometric growth
  (D) logistic growth

111. At point Z, Population 2 is

  (A) overshooting the environment's carrying capacity
  (B) growing exponentially
  (C) undergoing a population crash
  (D) experiencing logistic growth

112. After point Y, Population 1 will most likely

  (A) find a stable size at about 5,000
  (B) increase exponentially
  (C) experience a population crash
  (D) continue to fluctuate near its current level

113. Of the following, which is an example of a density-independent population control?

  (A) limited food
  (B) limited space
  (C) parasitism
  (D) earthquakes

114. When a population size tends to fluctuate around the environment's carrying capacity, biologists consider it to be

  (A) irruptive
  (B) stable
  (C) irregular
  (D) decaying

115. In contrast to humans, animals' fecundity is often very close to their

(A) life expectancy

(B) fertility

(C) life span

(D) survivorship

116. When the individuals of a population are most likely to be found in groups, their physical distribution is known as

(A) uniform dispersion

(B) exponential growth

(C) random dispersion

(D) clumping

117. The following factors contribute to an increase in a population's size:

I. births

II. immigration

III. emigration

(A) I only

(B) II only

(C) I and II

(D) II and III

118. When a population exceeds the environment's carrying capacity (K),

(A) it can suffer a sudden population crash

(B) it enters the exponential growth phase

(C) it overcomes environmental resistance

(D) its age structure becomes heavily weighted in favor of older individuals

119. When a population's growth adjusts to approximate the environment's carrying capacity (K), it is known as

(A) a species' biotic potential
(B) exponential growth
(C) a population crash
(D) logistic growth

120. One hundred mockingbirds live on a five-square-kilometer island, and in one year, they produce 20 offspring. In the same time, 10 birds die, and 30 birds immigrate. What is the island's new mockingbird population density?

(A) 150 individuals per square kilometer
(B) 140 individuals per square kilometer
(C) 28 individuals per square kilometer
(D) 16 individuals per square kilometer

121. If a population has high fecundity but low fertility,

(A) the current number of offspring is relatively low and is likely to stay low
(B) the current number of offspring is relatively high, but it is likely to decrease or stay the same
(C) the relative number of offspring is likely to increase and decrease wildly with time
(D) the current number of offspring is relatively low, but it may greatly increase

122. The scientific study of human populations is called demography. Demography focuses on how the population is structured, the size, and stages of development. One of these factors is the number of individuals per unit area. This is defined as

(A) density-dependent factors
(B) carrying capacity
(C) renewable resources
(D) population density

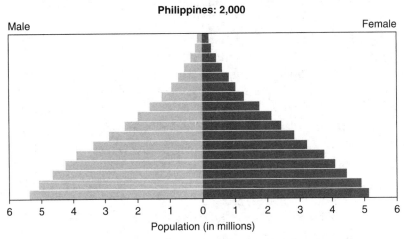

Philippines: 2,000

Source: U.S. Census Bureau, International Data Base

Figure 3.7

123. According to the age structure diagram in Figure 3.7, the population of this country is most likely

(A) growing slowly
(B) growing rapidly
(C) declining slowly
(D) declining rapidly

124. Which factors are found on an age structure pyramid?

(A) age and gender
(B) age and ethnicity
(C) ethnicity and gender
(D) ethnicity and illnesses

Male   **Female**

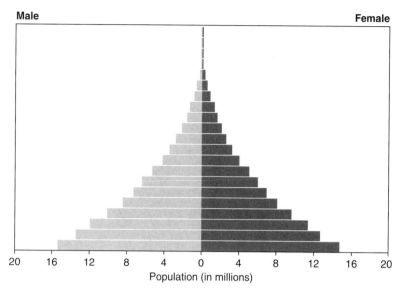

20   16   12   8   4   0   4   8   12   16   20
Population (in millions)

Figure 3.8

125. The population pyramid in Figure 3.8 most likely corresponds to which country's demographics?

(A) Japan
(B) Canada
(C) Nigeria
(D) Germany

126. An equation to estimate a human population's ecological impact uses the variables I (total impact), P (population size), A (population affluence), and T (population technology level). Using that equation, if P and A both double compared to a previous situation but T remains the same, what happens to I?

(A) I drops to zero.
(B) I drops to half its previous value.
(C) I remains the same value.
(D) I increases to four times its previous value.

127. A total fertility rate of 2.1 represents the average number of children born per woman at which a population stays the same from one generation to the next without migration. This is also defined as

(A) ultimate fertility rate
(B) total fertility rate
(C) replacement level fertility rate
(D) general fertility rate

128. Which country has the highest fertility rate in the world (as of 2019)?

(A) Niger
(B) China
(C) Singapore
(D) Japan

129. This term describes the number of years an individual is expected to live at the time it is born:

(A) life span
(B) fecundity
(C) fertility
(D) life expectancy

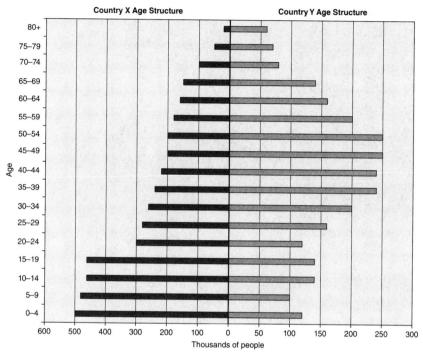

Figure 3.9

Questions 130–135 refer to the two age-structure graphs in Figure 3.9. Each represents the number of people of different age-groups living in a country at the same time.

130. Using only these graphs, it's possible to deduce that compared to Country Y, Country X currently has a higher

(A) emigration rate
(B) immigration rate
(C) birthrate
(D) intrinsic rate of increase

131. If Country Y is a typical developed nation, in 10 to 20 years it will begin suffering from

(A) a reduced tax base
(B) a high birthrate
(C) high population density
(D) low emigration

132. If Country X has recently industrialized, in 15 years its growth rate will most likely

(A) decrease
(B) increase
(C) remain the same
(D) fluctuate

133. Assuming its total population for the previous 200 years has been constant, Country X's population older than 20 years most closely reflects a survivorship curve showing

(A) early loss
(B) logistic growth
(C) constant loss
(D) logarithmic growth

134. Which country is most likely postindustrial?

(A) Country X
(B) Country Y
(C) neither
(D) both

135. Which of the following factors best explains Country Y's lower population in age brackets under 30 years old?

(A) emigration
(B) immigration
(C) a lower birthrate
(D) a higher death rate

136. In 1665, the Great Plague killed as many as 80,000 people in London, England, as plague-carrying fleas spread the disease among the city's inhabitants. The next year saw the Great Fire of London, which destroyed whole regions of the city and killed a reported six people—but probably a great many more. Some historians claim that the fire stopped plague-ridden fleas by killing their host rats by the thousands. Many historians believe that a "Little Ice Age" affected Northern Europe and other parts of the world, decreasing crop harvests and increasing instances of starvation and famine from about 1550 until about 1850.

(A) Was the Great Plague a density-independent or density-dependent factor affecting the human population of England?

(B) Which of the events mentioned above represent a density-independent factor affecting the human population?

(C) Which of the events mentioned above are abiotic factors, and which are biotic?

137. As demographers define it, industrial population growth includes

(A) high birthrates and high death rates

(B) high birthrates and low death rates

(C) low birthrates and high death rates

(D) low birthrates and low death rates

138. Demographers expect most developed nations to face challenges by the middle of this century involving which of the following?

  I. high birthrate

 II. rising death rate

III. high emigration

IV. negative growth

(A) I and II

(B) I and III

(C) II and III

(D) II and IV

139. Why is the replacement level fertility defined as 2.1 children per couple instead of just 2?

(A) Some people will die before reaching reproductive age.

(B) Developed countries use more birth control.

(C) Death rates are high in developing countries.

(D) Some people choose not to have children.

140. In 1798, Thomas Malthus hypothesized that the human population would reach and exceed its carrying capacity, and in turn, the population would collapse. Which of the following factors proved Malthus's hypothesis to be incorrect and has led to an increase in the human population?

(A) the increased use of fossil fuels worldwide

(B) reliance on renewable energy

(C) the creation of the polio vaccine

(D) food production increases via the Green Revolution

141. Some countries in Europe have a lower infant mortality rate than the United States in part because of which of the following?

(A) increased sexual education for teenagers

(B) high suicide rate of teens

(C) more teenage pregnancies

(D) decreased use of contraceptives and fewer live births for teens

142. Which of the following is the correct order of demographic states that a country experiences when industrializing?

(A) nomadic → pre-industrial → industrial → post-industrial

(B) Iron Age → agrarian → pre-industrial → industrial

(C) nomadic → agrarian → pre-industrial → industrial

(D) pre-industrial → transitional → industrial → post-industrial

Use Figure 3.10 for Questions 143–144.

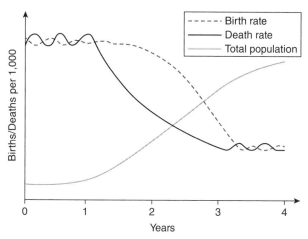

Human Demographic Transition

Figure 3.10

143. In what stage of the demographic transition would the birth rate and death rate both be the highest?
(A) Stage 1
(B) Stage 2
(C) Stage 3
(D) Stage 4

144. Which stage of the demographic transition model is considered to be ideal since total population growth is gradual over time?
(A) Stage 1
(B) Stage 2
(C) Stage 3
(D) Stage 4

145. The United States is in which stage of the demographic transition?
(A) Stage 1
(B) Stage 2
(C) Stage 3
(D) Stage 4

146. If 20,000 of a small country's total population of 1 million live in cities, the country's degree of urbanization is

(A) 20%

(B) 5%

(C) 2%

(D) 0.2%

147. If a country maintains the same total population of 100 million but its rural population shrinks from 55% to 52% in one year, what is the urban growth rate for this period, assuming that the rest of the population is composed of city dwellers?

(A) 2.7%

(B) 6.7%

(C) 3.0%

(D) 0.9%

148. All of the following statements are examples of the negative effects of urban sprawl EXCEPT

(A) an increase in automobile traffic

(B) the loss of central city tax bases

(C) the loss of prime cropland, grass, and forests

(D) decreased water runoff

149. Of the following statements, which one accurately reflects current urban growth patterns worldwide?

(A) Urban growth is slower in developed countries than in developing countries.

(B) Urban poverty is becoming less prevalent.

(C) City dwellers are staying at a constant percentage of the world population.

(D) In developing countries, the rural population is becoming a greater proportion of the population.

150. People can be "pulled" to emigrate from rural areas into urban areas by

(A) poverty in rural areas

(B) lack of agricultural land outside of cities

(C) lack of jobs outside of cities

(D) available housing in urban areas

CHAPTER 4

Earth Systems and Resources

151. Magma fills the gap between tectonic plates, forming new crust at

(A) subsidence zones

(B) subduction zones

(C) sedimentation zones

(D) divergent faults

152. Earthquakes release huge amounts of energy accumulated through which of the following processes?

(A) tectonic plates constantly pushing against one another

(B) compressed magma being forced to the surface through cracks and vents

(C) the relentless back-and-forth movement of ocean tides

(D) sudden heating of the earth's core

153. Which three processes are needed in order to convert metamorphic or igneous rock into sedimentary rock?

(A) heating, pressure, and stress

(B) erosion, heating, and transportation

(C) pressure, erosion, and heat

(D) weathering, erosion, and deposition

154. Using the Richter scale, an earthquake of magnitude 5.0 is how many times more powerful than an earthquake of magnitude 4.0?

(A) 1.25

(B) 5

(C) 10

(D) 50

155. Subduction zones tend to produce deep undersea trenches as a result of

(A) two tectonic plates moving directly away from each other

(B) two tectonic plates sliding past each other

(C) one tectonic plate being pulled apart at the center

(D) one tectonic plate being forced to bend under another

156. Tsunamis, like the one that hit northeastern Japan in March 2011, are usually caused by

(A) magma suddenly released into the ocean

(B) earthquakes under the ocean floor

(C) rapid closing of an ocean trench

(D) subsidence of land near the ocean

157. If a nearby city experiences earthquake damage of intensity XI, the earthquake's Richter scale magnitude is most likely to be

(A) 0.9 or less

(B) 1.0 to 2.9

(C) 3.0 to 4.9

(D) 7.0 or greater

158. Volcanoes can spew several types of gas, but the two main components are

   I. oxygen gas

  II. carbon dioxide

 III. hydrogen gas

 IV. hydrogen sulfide

  V. water vapor

(A) I and II

(B) II and III

(C) III and IV

(D) II and V

159. In which of the following environments are laterite soils more likely to form?

(A) grasslands

(B) tundra

(C) conifer forests

(D) tropics

160. Coastal wetlands are ecologically important because they do all of the following EXCEPT

(A) reduce the impact of storms coming inland

(B) harbor a high level of biodiversity

(C) help to cycle nutrients

(D) offer an important refuge for large marine mammals

161. Volcanoes tend to occur nearest to

(A) the centers of tectonic plates

(B) the highest points along the equator

(C) ancient meteor impact sites

(D) the boundaries of tectonic plates

162. Which of the following ocean zones contains the greatest total number of producers?

(A) the euphotic zone
(B) the bathyal zone
(C) the abyssal zone
(D) the coastal zone

163. To the west and southwest of Wyoming's Yellowstone National Park, there is evidence of several volcanic eruptions that have occurred over the past 17 million years. Today, the park has many features associated with volcanically active areas, including hot springs and geysers. But Yellowstone lies well within the North American plate. There are huge, mostly flat regions in the area around Yellowstone, where mountains once stood. These areas formed during huge volcanic eruptions, and they are oval or nearly circular in shape.

(A) What is the likely cause of volcanoes in the Yellowstone region over the past 17 million years?
(B) In which direction is the North American plate moving?
(C) What is the name of the large flat areas left by ancient volcanoes, and what causes them?

164. Currently, the atmosphere surrounding earth is composed mainly of

(A) nitrogen
(B) oxygen
(C) carbon dioxide
(D) helium

165. The Coriolis effect

(A) changes the circulation direction of water running down a drain
(B) changes the direction of river flow
(C) changes the direction of winds all around earth
(D) causes winds in the Northern Hemisphere to move to the east

166. Temperatures within the stratosphere increase with elevation due to the presence of

(A) the ozone layer
(B) numerous clouds
(C) high-speed winds
(D) temperature inversion

167. The Coriolis effect is the result of

(A) earth's gravitational pull
(B) earth's rotation on its axis
(C) the gravitational pull of the moon
(D) the revolution of earth around the sun

168. An isobar on a weather map connects areas of

(A) low pressure
(B) high pressure
(C) equal elevation
(D) equal atmospheric pressure

169. Which statement best describes physical weathering?

(A) the breaking of a bigger rock into smaller pieces with a change in chemical composition
(B) the breaking of a bigger rock into smaller pieces without a change in chemical composition
(C) the compaction and cementation of sediment into a sedimentary rock
(D) the gradual cooling of magma into an igneous rock

170. The chemical weathering process of hydrolysis breaks down a rock that reacts with

(A) oxygen
(B) carbonic acid
(C) percarbonic acid
(D) water

171. Plants, mosses, and bacteria break down rocks through

(A) chemical weathering
(B) exfoliation
(C) unloading
(D) both physical weathering and chemical weathering

Use Figure 4.1 to answer questions 172–174.

172. Which layer in the soil horizon serves as the parent material for the soil that forms?

(A) Horizon O
(B) Horizon A
(C) Horizon B
(D) Bedrock

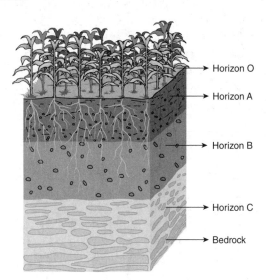

Figure 4.1

173. The topsoil is composed of

(A) Horizon O
(B) Horizon A
(C) Horizon B
(D) Horizons O and A

174. Horizon B is also sometimes referred to as the

(A) zone of accumulation
(B) zone of leaching
(C) parent materials
(D) topsoil

175. Pedocal soils are characterized by large accumulations of

(A) iron oxide
(B) calcium carbonate
(C) aluminum-rich clay
(D) organic material

176. How does the amount of water warm air can hold compare to the amount of water colder air can hold?

(A) Warm air can hold more water than cold air.
(B) Warm air can hold less water than cold air.
(C) Warm air and cold air can hold the same amount of water.
(D) Warm air is not able to hold water, and cold air is.

177. Erosion may occur due to the repeated freeze-and-thaw cycle in some climates. This process is called

(A) granular disintegration
(B) joint block separation
(C) frost wedging
(D) unloading

178. In which layer of the earth's atmosphere would you find ultraviolet (UV) protection from the ozone layer?

(A) troposphere
(B) stratosphere
(C) mesosphere
(D) exosphere

179. Which layer of the earth's atmosphere protects us from extreme ultraviolet radiation and reflects radio waves?

(A) troposphere
(B) stratosphere
(C) mesosphere
(D) ionosphere

180. Which gas is the most abundant in earth's atmosphere?

(A) oxygen
(B) hydrogen
(C) nitrogen
(D) helium

181. What causes the deflection of objects traveling long distances above the earth's surface, referred to as the Coriolis effect?

(A) the curvature of the earth's surface
(B) effects of winds high in the atmosphere
(C) revolution of the earth around the sun
(D) rotation of the earth on its axis

182. Referred to as the rain shadow effect, on which side of mountains are deserts often found?

(A) windward side
(B) leeward side
(C) western edge
(D) eastern edge

183. Which type of atmospheric wind patterns would you find at 0°–30° latitude (north and south)?

(A) polar cells
(B) convection cells
(C) westerlies
(D) Hadley cells

184. What is the name of the phenomenon that causes air masses to rise and sink with uneven heating and cooling and drives our global wind patterns?

(A) Coriolis effect
(B) convention
(C) subduction
(D) circulation

185. African dust storms begin in the Sahara Desert, where wind storms blow desert dust thousands of feet into the atmosphere. Dust clouds that can be thousands of miles long, travel west on wind patterns, across both the Atlantic Ocean and Caribbean Seas. Which major wind pattern drives the dust storms?

(A) westerlies
(B) polar currents
(C) northeast trades
(D) trade winds

186. The fast-moving air currents can transport weather systems across the United States, affecting temperature and precipitation.

(A) doldrums
(B) westerlies
(C) the jet stream
(D) subtropical highs

187. What water management technique is used to control floods and erosion, improve drainage, and improve navigation?

(A) catchwater system
(B) condensation
(C) overdraft
(D) channelization

188. *Dendritic drainage* is

(A) percolation of water into groundwater
(B) a branching drainage pattern of streams
(C) seeping of water out of discharge zones
(D) evapotranspiration from plants

189. The type of soil in the watershed impacts the amount of runoff absorbed by soil as well as the vegetation. Which type of soil composition would provide the best water drainage because it has more space in between the particles?

(A) sand
(B) loam
(C) clay
(D) sandy clay

190. Where is the largest aquifer in the world located?

(A) Canada
(B) the United States
(C) Russia
(D) Zambia

191. The Atlantic hurricane season lasts from June 1 to November 30. Some climate models predict that hurricanes will become more common each year. Others indicate that the number of Atlantic hurricanes may fluctuate each year but remain fairly constant in the long term.

(A) Why is the Atlantic hurricane season limited to the period between June and November? What conditions can cause a hurricane to occur?
(B) How might climate change cause hurricanes to become more common?
(C) What evidence contradicts the view that climate change will cause more hurricanes?

192. Most places on earth experience distinct seasons featuring differences in temperature and precipitation. Earth is not the only planet in the solar system with seasons, although the changes in seasons are marked by different phenomena elsewhere.

(A) What causes earth's seasons?

(B) The earth and the sun are closer during the Northern Hemisphere's winter than during its summer. Explain how this is possible.

(C) How do the seasons impact the climate of particular locations on earth?

193. Different biomes experience seasonal differences throughout the year. Some areas experience all four seasons, while others only experience two distinct seasons. What is the cause of the different seasons?

(A) climate change

(B) the distance from the sun

(C) the tilt of the earth on its axis

(D) the gravitational pull of the moon

194. Insolation is defined as the amount of solar radiation reaching a given area. How does the atmosphere interfere with insolation?

(A) The atmosphere does not interfere with the solar radiation.

(B) Energy is reflected, absorbed, and scattered by atmospheric gases.

(C) Solar radiation burns off the gases in the atmosphere.

(D) Most of the solar radiation can't travel through the atmosphere.

195. Trade winds in the Northern and Southern Hemispheres deflect toward

(A) the equator

(B) the poles

(C) continental landmasses

(D) the temperate zones

196. How does the climate in a region differ from its weather?

(A) Climate is a larger land area.

(B) Climate is all of the surrounding weather combined.

(C) Climate is the average of the daily weather over a long period of time.

(D) Weather is not a scientific measurement.

197. Which two variables are most responsible for climate differences on earth?

(A) temperature and altitude

(B) precipitation and temperature

(C) precipitation and water sources

(D) temperature and soil type

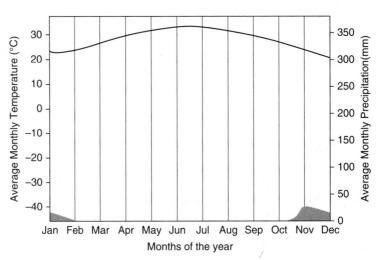

Figure 4.2

198. Which of the following biomes is most likely represented by the climatogram in Figure 4.2?

(A) taiga

(B) tundra

(C) desert

(D) tropical rainforest

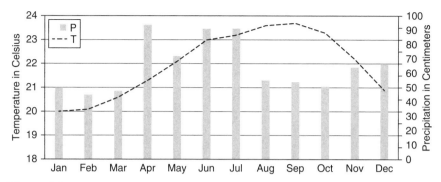

Figure 4.3

199. Which of the following biomes is most likely represented by the climatogram in Figure 4.3?

(A) temperate deciduous forest
(B) tundra
(C) desert
(D) tropical rainforest

200. An increase in elevation causes a change in biomes. Which of the following statements is caused by a change in elevation (like up the side of a mountain)?

(A) As you go up in elevation, biomes become more diverse because of the colder temperatures.
(B) Precipitation increases as air rises, and water vapor condenses into clouds, resulting in vegetation that requires more moisture to grow.
(C) The land becomes arid, resulting in the growth of different types of drought-intolerant vegetation.
(D) As elevation decreases, the precipitation increases because you are closer to the ocean.

201. Sunspot activity directly affects the temperature within the

(A) thermosphere
(B) mesosphere
(C) ionosphere
(D) stratosphere

202. Which two factors allow earth to experience four distinct seasons?

(A) latitude, solar intensity

(B) tilt of axis, rotation on axis

(C) tilt of axis, revolution around sun

(D) distance from sun, revolution around sun

203. Hurricanes begin with

(A) a drop in temperature

(B) periods of wind shear

(C) a drop in barometric pressure

(D) incoming tides

204. Relative humidity is a measurement of

(A) temperature of the air and elevation

(B) elevation and the amount of water vapor in the air

(C) the amount of water vapor the air can hold and latitude

(D) air temperature and the amount of water vapor in the air

205. Temperature inversions within the troposphere are likely to occur in association with

(A) oceans

(B) deserts

(C) urban areas

(D) mountain ranges

206. Which of the following is a characteristic of the troposphere?

(A) part of the atmosphere that contains the ozone layer

(B) an increase of temperature with elevation

(C) the aurora borealis

(D) layer where our weather occurs

207. On average, an El Niño–Southern Oscillation (ENSO) event occurs every

(A) 1 to 2 years
(B) 2 to 7 years
(C) 7 to 10 years
(D) 15 to 25 years

208. Which of the following is characteristic of an El Niño year?

(A) Warm water in the Pacific is pushed westward.
(B) Cold water upwells along the South American coast.
(C) Warm water flows eastward, reaching South America.
(D) Cold water in the Pacific is pushed westward.

209. What is the difference between an El Niño event and a La Niña event?

(A) La Niña involves cool Pacific Ocean surface temperatures, while El Niño involves warmer ocean surface temperatures.
(B) El Niño is a milder version of La Niña.
(C) La Niña events occur in the Pacific Ocean, and El Niño events occur in the Atlantic Ocean.
(D) La Niña events occur in the Atlantic Ocean, and El Niño events occur in the Pacific Ocean.

210. The global impact of an ENSO includes all of the following EXCEPT

(A) drought in the western Pacific
(B) flooding in the eastern Pacific
(C) disruption of the fish population along South America
(D) an increase in the number of Atlantic hurricanes

CHAPTER 5

Land and Water Use

211. One approach to building more efficient housing with recreational space involves concentrating high-density housing in one part of a site and leaving a large proportion for shared open space. This is known as

(A) fundamental land
(B) land-use planning
(C) smart growth
(D) cluster development

212. Officially created in 1872, Yellowstone National Park was the first of 58 national parks in the United States and the first national park in the world. Its 8,987 square kilometers (or 3,472 square miles) contain breathtaking beauty, natural wonders, and habitats featuring grizzly bears, bison, and rare thermophilic bacteria. About 80% of Yellowstone is covered by forest, with 15% devoted to grassland and 5% devoted to water.

(A) Why did the United States first establish national parks such as Yellowstone?
(B) How do parks help to preserve endangered and rare species?
(C) What U.S. agency administers the country's national parks?
(D) What are some of the chief threats to national parks?

213. Which of the following are examples of "the tragedy of the commons"?

(A) overfishing and earthquake damage
(B) deforestation and overfishing
(C) pollution and overpopulation
(D) viral outbreaks

214. Which method of timber harvesting cuts a small percentage of mature trees every 10 to 20 years?

(A) clear-cutting
(B) deforestation
(C) selective cutting
(D) old-growth harvesting

215. The country that has the largest area of old-growth forest in the world is

(A) China
(B) Brazil
(C) Canada
(D) the United States

216. Which of the following is considered to be a benefit of clear-cutting a section of the forest?

(A) soil erosion
(B) decrease in biodiversity
(C) increase in carbon dioxide emissions
(D) most efficient and economical

217. After about a century of logging, deforestation in Madagascar's rain forests and its mangroves on the coast have left the country with terrible erosion problems. Slash-and-burn agricultural practices have turned a once verdant island into one with some of the fastest-changing coastlines—sediment washes down Madagascar's large rivers and fills coastal waterways on its way to the ocean. According to NASA, astronauts say it looks like the country is "bleeding" after heavy rain washes its red soil out to sea.

(A) How is the nitrogen cycle on Madagascar likely affected by its deforestation?

(B) How is the hydrologic cycle on Madagascar likely affected?

(C) How is the biological carbon cycle on Madagascar likely affected?

218. The difference between drought and degradation of land is

(A) degradation is not affected by climate

(B) degradation results from unsound human activities

(C) drought is an unnatural event

(D) degradation increases economic yield

219. Desertification is occurring in many parts of the world due to the impact of people and climate change.

(A) Describe three signs of desertification in an area.

(B) Describe two specific examples of how people have contributed to desertification.

(C) Describe alternative methods that could be used instead of the ones that were described in (B).

220. *Silent Spring* is a book published in 1962 that warned of the impact of

(A) deforestation in the Amazon

(B) pesticides and herbicides

(C) nuclear war

(D) population growth

221. What makes grasslands so suitable for agriculture?

(A) They are flat and easier to plow.

(B) High-quality soil results from a deep organic layer.

(C) There is a large area available in the world.

(D) There are no animals that eat the grasses.

222. This type of farming practice plants one family of crops one year and a different family of crops the next year, doing so for several years in a row. This farming method is critical in replenishing soil nutrients naturally and avoiding pest issues that affect monocultures. This process is known as

(A) contour farming

(B) ecological revolution

(C) biological integration

(D) crop rotation

223. Which of the following is NOT a way that agriculture affects the environment?

(A) changing of land cover

(B) carbon dioxide emission from agriculture industry

(C) runoff of pesticides into rivers and streams

(D) increase of biological diversity

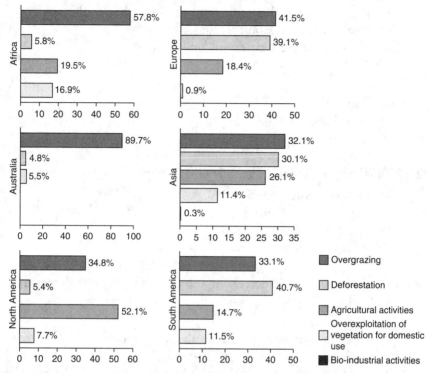

Figure 5.1

224. According to the graphic in Figure 5.1, which land-use issue has the largest impact on desertification in the world?

(A) overgrazing (animals)
(B) deforestation
(C) agricultural activities (farming)
(D) overexploitation of vegetation for domestic use

225. Feedlots are damaging to the environment because of

(A) overgrazing
(B) deforestation
(C) erosion
(D) pollution

226. Which of the following is true about people in China?

    I. They are consuming more meat products than in the past.

    II. More grain production is required.

    III. China has more agricultural land available now than in the past.

    (A) I only

    (B) II only

    (C) I and II only

    (D) II and III only

227. Which of these crops are mainly GMO crops?

    (A) soybeans, cotton, and corn

    (B) wheat, rice, and corn

    (C) wheat, cotton, and corn

    (D) potatoes, wheat, and rice

228. Overfishing is quickly decreasing the world's supply of fish, which would greatly impact the availability of protein to developing nations.

    (A) Describe two fishing methods that contribute to the problem of overfishing.

    (B) Describe two methods that would help prevent overfishing.

229. Topsoil, the layer of soil that supports crops, is also known as the

    (A) litter layer

    (B) A horizon

    (C) zone of accumulation

    (D) C horizon

230. An agricultural field that is NOT harvested for at least a season is

    (A) subsidized

    (B) terraced

    (C) contoured

    (D) fallow

231. Using reclaimed water, preventing runoff, and using dry cooling systems in industrial processes are all methods of

(A) precipitation

(B) conservation

(C) groundwater mining

(D) aquifer recharge

232. All the land from which water drains to a common lake or river is considered to be part of the same

(A) watershed

(B) aquifer

(C) runoff zone

(D) both A and C

233. Resources such as groundwater that are being consumed faster than they can be resupplied are said to be

(A) infiltrated

(B) highly salinized

(C) in the zone of saturation

(D) nonrenewable

234. The boundary between the zone of saturation and zone of aeration is known as the

(A) watershed

(B) water table

(C) aquifer recharge zone

(D) runoff

235. The ideal method of irrigation for water conservation is

(A) flood irrigation

(B) ditch irrigation

(C) sprinkler irrigation

(D) drip irrigation

236. Which of the following illustrates a water budget?

(A) water volume − surface area = total % of water
(B) stream flow − subsurface flow = evaporation
(C) precipitation − evaporation = runoff
(D) precipitation − consumptive use = water available

237. Agriculture that alternates two or more crops to reduce wind and water erosion is known as

(A) terracing
(B) shelterbelts
(C) soil compaction
(D) strip cropping

238. Current farming methods typically use one of two approaches: conventional or sustainable agriculture.

(A) How do conventional agriculture and sustainable agriculture differ in their approaches to controlling weeds, suppressing insect pests, and adding nutrients to the soil?
(B) Describe and explain three ways that conventional agriculture disrupts the natural ecology of an area.
(C) Describe three sustainable agriculture techniques that avoid disruption of land.

239. The types of crops that are used directly by a farmer or sold locally are

(A) cash crops
(B) ruminant crops
(C) subsistence crops
(D) monoculture crops

240. Which of the following types of crops have the benefits of conserving soil, retaining nutrients, and saving energy?

(A) annual crops
(B) cash crops
(C) subsistence crops
(D) perennial crops

241. The optimal growth of a crop can be prevented by a shortage in the soil of a chemical element known as

(A) a macronutrient
(B) a micronutrient
(C) a limiting factor
(D) a fumigant

242. Herbicides account for what percentage of pesticides in U.S. waters?

(A) 80%
(B) 10%
(C) 60%
(D) 5%

243. Rangeland covers approximately 70% of the earth's surface, yet most of it is in poor condition. Grazing practices are responsible for much of the degradation.

(A) Compare and contrast traditional herding of cattle with industrial methods of raising cattle.
(B) Describe two effects of introducing nonnative grazing animals to an area of rangeland.
(C) You have inherited the family cattle business from your grandfather in Texas. You want to run the business in a sustainable way. Describe five methods you can use to make the business more ecologically sound.

244. Which of the following fishing methods is characterized by "enclosing a school of fish with a large net"?

(A) long-line fishing
(B) drift-net fishing
(C) trawling
(D) purse-seine fishing

245. One of the side effects of large-scale fishing methods such as trawling is catching species that you do not want or need. This causes those species to be killed and just thrown back into the ocean. What is the name of the phenomenon of catching unintended and unwanted species?

(A) ghost fishing
(B) long-lining
(C) bycatch
(D) riparian destruction

246. In 2009, the PacRim mining company proposed its Chuitna Coal Project in Alaska—a strip mine and associated development that together would cover about 78 square kilometers (about 30 square miles) of the Beluga Coal Fields near the Cook Inlet southwest of Anchorage. Many activists, residents, and fishery experts are concerned that although the company is taking some steps to reduce waste released, the mine will destroy area streams, which are important salmon hatcheries that contribute to the local economy. Mine proponents estimate that the 25-year first phase of the project could create as many as 350 new jobs and stimulate the local economy by involving local businesses. The company also plans to create a major port nearby that could encourage further development of the area, as well as further mining.

(A) What is strip mining?
(B) How might strip mining endanger streams and the salmon inhabiting them?
(C) At what point would the Surface Mining Control and Reclamation Act of 1977 require PacRim to attempt some environmental restoration?

247. The process of using water to wash soil and other unwanted materials to reveal desired minerals is known as

(A) strip mining
(B) smelting
(C) heap-leach extraction
(D) placer mining

248. In 2011, the Australian government produced a report on urbanization suggesting that development in the country should concentrate on filling in urban areas, particularly in derelict sites. Inner cities, said the report, should be connected to transport corridors and green spaces to provide a high standard of living in a more efficient manner. At the same time, Prime Minister Julia Gillard promised to increase job opportunities in outer suburbs, which have fewer community services, such as health, education, and housing facilities.

(A) In the paragraph above, which stated goal is likely to increase urban sprawl?

(B) How might filling in urban areas allow people to experience a high standard of living more efficiently?

(C) How might urban areas with more community services better survive economic fluctuations?

249. Flooding is often a bigger problem in cities than in rural areas due to which of the following factors?

I. Cities are often built in coastal areas or on floodplains.

II. Cities' greater proportion of impervious cover increases runoff.

III. City-related development often damages wetlands that can absorb excess water.

IV. Cities release excess heat and carbon dioxide, which increase local rainfall.

(A) I and II only

(B) II and III only

(C) I and IV only

(D) I, II, and III

250. Sewage runoff from human settlements into the oceans can cause all of the following EXCEPT

(A) harmful algal blooms

(B) exposure of marine life and people to high levels of infectious bacteria

(C) unusually high levels of human viruses in the water

(D) calcium-rich zones that damage fish and shellfish by hardening and stiffening joints

251. Transit corridors connect cities such as Toronto to smaller nearby urbanized areas, with the rest of the area surrounding the city center devoted to recreational open space known as
    (A) fundamental land
    (B) mixed-use zoning
    (C) greenbelt
    (D) cluster development

252. Urban planning experts call a neighborhood with stores, light industries, offices, high-density housing, and mass transportation within walking distance
    (A) a mixed-use development
    (B) smart-growth planning
    (C) cluster development
    (D) reconciliation ecology

253. In the United States, urban sprawl was encouraged by the federal government through
    I. loan guarantees for veterans buying new single-family homes
    II. federal funding of highways
    III. the introduction of home-loan deductions for federal income tax
    IV. large federally funded suburban developments outside western U.S. cities
    (A) I, II, and III
    (B) II, III, and IV
    (C) I, III, and IV
    (D) I and II only

254. Cities can put extra stress on the environment's water resources by
  I. depriving nearby, less-developed areas of surface water and groundwater
  II. decreasing the amount of groundwater by increasing runoff
  III. decreasing nearby cloud formation by producing excess heat and CO_2
  IV. contributing to water pollution
  (A) I, II, and III
  (B) II, III, and IV
  (C) I, II, and IV
  (D) I and III only

255. Approximately what percentage of crops are destroyed by pests, spoilage, and disease?
  (A) 30%
  (B) 10%
  (C) 50%
  (D) 20%

256. Using excess groundwater in coastal regions causes
  (A) a sustainable water supply
  (B) condensation nuclei
  (C) surface water to decline
  (D) both C and D

257. Building and construction sites mainly affect water purity by
  (A) producing loose sediment that washes away in heavy rainfall
  (B) producing hazardous chemicals that infiltrate groundwater
  (C) creating more evaporation of groundwater
  (D) groundwater mining of local resources

258. An influent stream is

(A) entirely above the water table
(B) a result of precipitation
(C) maintained by groundwater seeping in
(D) both A and B

259. When groundwater is removed, the soil sinks in a process known as

(A) saturation
(B) stabilization
(C) subsidence
(D) streambed channelization

260. In the wake of Hurricane Katrina, you have been appointed to a special committee by the government to look at ways to prevent flooding in other cities in the future.

(A) Discuss how both natural events and man-made changes contribute to flooding.
(B) Describe two methods of flood control that are currently in use in the United States and the drawbacks of each.
(C) The Watershed Protection and Flood Prevention Act of 1954 was intended to alleviate the problem of flooding where wetlands were located. Explain whether or not this legislation was effective and why or why not.
(D) Outline your recommendations to the government, using the concept of watershed management.

261. Which of the following methods use biological control to combat pest issues?

(A) using windbreaks
(B) using pesticides that travel through waterways
(C) bringing in natural enemies such as predators, parasites, and bacteria
(D) synthetic pesticides

262. Which of the following would be a disadvantage of using pesticides to deal with crop pests?

(A) Pesticides will not degrade quickly.
(B) Pests become resistant to the pesticides over time.
(C) Pesticides decrease the cost of food due to the lack of loss of crops.
(D) Pesticides can save human lives when killing pests such as mosquitos.

263. One of the methods farmers use to prevent soil erosion is a practice called *terracing*. Which of the following best describes this practice?

(A) plowing fields perpendicular to the slope of hills
(B) leaving old stalks and other plant material on fields
(C) planting alfalfa or clover on fields
(D) converting large, steep fields into smaller fields

264. What is a benefit of contour plowing?

(A) an increase in soil fertility
(B) a slowdown in runoff
(C) a decrease in windblown soil
(D) water forms deep pools

265. Which of the following events have contributed to an increased impact on the environment?

a. human use of tools
b. human disease and famine
c. technological advancements
d. industrial revolution

(A) A and B
(B) A and C
(C) A, B, and C
(D) A, C, and D

266. Which of the following is NOT a public service function of forests?

(A) slowing of erosion
(B) increasing evaporation of water
(C) providing recreational activities
(D) providing timber

267. Indirect deforestation is

(A) death of trees from pollution or disease
(B) killing some trees unintentionally during selective cutting
(C) loss of trees from logging
(D) cutting of forests by local people for fuel

268. When a forest is harvested at a rate that does NOT decrease supply year after year, it is said to be

(A) clear-cut
(B) sustainable
(C) old-growth
(D) suppressed

269. Which of the following are benefits of forest fires?

I. pinecones open and release seeds
II. removal of brush and replenishment of soils
III. increasing the number of crown fires

(A) I only
(B) II only
(C) I and II only
(D) II and III only

270. Minimum tillage is a farming technique that

(A) decreases the use of herbicides
(B) increases soil compaction
(C) reduces soil erosion
(D) increases evaporation of water

CHAPTER 6

Energy Resources and Consumption

271. Which three of the following are renewable energy sources?

   I. biomass
   II. natural gas
   III. coal
   IV. hydropower
   V. oil
   VI. solar power

(A) I, II, and VI
(B) I, IV, and VI
(C) II, IV, and VI
(D) II, III, and V

272. Compared with conventional petroleum oil, the amount of carbon dioxide released by burning unconventional oils is

(A) about one-tenth as large
(B) about half as large
(C) about the same
(D) about twice as large

273. Of the following lists of the world's energy supplies, which begins with the supply that is likely to last longest and ends with the supply that will likely run out soonest?

(A) solar, conventional oil, natural gas
(B) solar, natural gas, conventional oil
(C) coal, solar, conventional oil
(D) conventional oil, natural gas, coal

274. The Bog of Allen in Ireland is an ancient lake that gradually began filling with plant matter about 10,000 years ago and is now completely filled. As plant matter accumulated, it was pushed to the bottom of the lake and compressed, eventually undergoing slow chemical reactions that changed it into peat. For thousands of years, people living in the area have burned peat from the bog for fuel, and starting in the 1900s, peat production became an industrialized process. About 90% of the bog is now dry or has been removed for use as fuel. Other ancient wetlands have managed to maintain a thin layer of water for a very long time, allowing peat to accumulate for hundreds of thousands of years, due to gradual sinking of the land or gradual rising of the water level as plant matter accumulates. In these places, sediment occasionally washes over the peat to compress it further, and peat at the bottom of the heap slowly turns into coal. Peat has a carbon content of about 60% when dry, while anthracite coal has a carbon content of about 87%.

(A) Is peat a fossil fuel or a renewable fuel?
(B) How does the carbon content of bituminous coal compare to that of peat and anthracite coal?
(C) Is peat from the Bog of Allen likely to ever become coal?

275. Canada has large deposits—about three-fourths of the world's supply—of an unconventional oil known as

(A) bitumen, or tar sands
(B) shale oil, or kerogen oil
(C) biomass-based liquid supplies
(D) coal-based liquid supplies

276. Most of the world's oil is located beneath countries in

(A) South America
(B) the Far East
(C) Europe
(D) the Middle East

277. Which of the following heating methods involves the most efficient conversion from its naturally occurring form to heat?

(A) whale oil burned in an old-fashioned lantern
(B) sunlight through the window absorbed by the walls of a room
(C) heating oil in a house's furnace
(D) sunlight collected by a solar panel to run an electric heater

278. All of the following are typically derived from fossil fuels EXCEPT

(A) geothermal power
(B) plastics
(C) organic chemicals
(D) U.S. electrical power

279. When energy extractors find it underground, "natural gas" is a mixture of gases, but it's mostly composed of

(A) butane
(B) propane
(C) methane
(D) ethane

280. The one major pollutant released by burning natural gas is

(A) mercury
(B) hydrogen sulfide
(C) hydrogen cyanide
(D) carbon dioxide

281. Contour strip mining is a method specialized to extract coal in terrain that is

(A) hilly or mountainous
(B) generally flat
(C) underwater
(D) covered with swamps or marshland

282. Transporting natural gas can be expensive for which two of the following reasons?
  I. It requires the building and maintenance of special pipelines.
  II. It must be cooled to a very low temperature to liquefy for shipping.
  III. It must undergo hydraulic fracturing to prepare it for fuel use.
  IV. It must be purified of radioactive contaminants before it can be transported.
  (A) I and II
  (B) I and III
  (C) II and III
  (D) II and IV

283. A company called General Fusion aims to build a working model of a novel type of fusion reactor by 2033. The reactor involves a spinning sphere of liquid metal—lead and lithium—with a hollow internal cylinder maintained by the constant rotation. Inside the hollow chamber is a magnetically suspended deuterium-tritium fuel, which is compressed about one time every second by pistons hammering on the outside layer of the spinning metal sphere. The resulting compression wave is supposed to cause brief nuclear fusion. This reaction releases neutrons that are slowed down by the metal, which heats up. Some hot metal is extracted to create electricity.
  (A) What are deuterium and tritium?
  (B) Why is the plasma magnetically suspended rather than kept in a solid container of some sort?
  (C) How does General Fusion probably plan to generate electricity using hot metal?

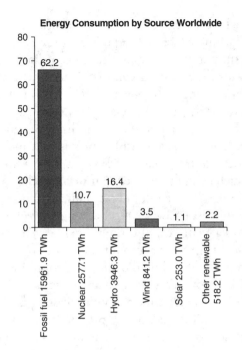

Figure 6.1

284. According to Figure 6.1, which source is the second most used global energy resource (as of 2015)?

(A) nuclear
(B) hydroelectric
(C) wind
(D) solar

285. Which country is the greatest user of nuclear power in the world?

(A) France
(B) United States
(C) Russia
(D) China

286. When global demand for oil exceeds the rate at which it is actually produced,

(A) the flow rate is stopped
(B) oil prices and demand don't change
(C) oil prices decrease because the demand increases
(D) the flow rate to consumers decreases and the price goes up

287. In the United States, energy experts have been contemplating the benefits of turning coal into a liquid fuel to replace petroleum-based fuels such as gasoline and diesel. According to the American Association for the Advancement of Science, the justification for coal-to-oil approaches is to prepare for higher oil prices and to reduce U.S. dependence on foreign petroleum. There are two basic ways to turn coal into a liquid fuel—indirect liquefaction and direct liquefaction. The first is a multistep process in which production facilities turn coal into a gas called syngas; they then remove impurities such as sulfur and refine it into diesel or gasoline fuels. According to AAAS, the full indirect liquefaction process is three to four times more expensive than processing the same amount of oil, and it releases a great deal of carbon dioxide even before the fuel is burned. When taking into account the cost of new infrastructure and the capturing of carbon dioxide released during refinement, indirect liquefaction becomes more expensive still. In the second major procedure, direct liquefaction, processing facilities use high-temperature chemical reactions to produce a liquid fuel. This fuel is currently used in China, but it contains many impurities that prevent complete combustion, resulting in emissions of unburned fuel as well as other impurities that make it illegal to use in the United States. As a result, its equivalent per-barrel price is even higher than that of fuel produced by indirect liquefaction.

(A) How does the second law of thermodynamics increase the price of energy from coal-derived liquid fuel?

(B) What factors might encourage U.S. adoption of coal-derived liquid fuel?

(C) What are the likely negative effects of the incomplete combustion of fuel derived from direct coal liquefaction?

(D) Even if coal-derived liquid fuel is highly refined and the process is made emission-free, what major environmental risks would it still produce?

288. Processing biomass with bacteria can produce which three of the following fuels?

   I. methane
  II. methanol
 III. ethanol
 IV. hydrogen
  V. butane
 VI. charcoal

(A) I, II, and III
(B) I, III, and IV
(C) II, III, and IV
(D) II, IV, and V

289. Which of the following is the LEAST efficient way to use energy stored in biomass?

(A) directly burning it to produce heat in an open fire
(B) converting it to gas to burn for heat
(C) converting it to ethanol for use as an automobile fuel
(D) burning it to run a steam turbine for electricity to make hydrogen from water for automobile fuel

290. Of the following materials, which CANNOT be used as a biomass fuel?

(A) charcoal
(B) granite
(C) animal dung
(D) cardboard

291. The three largest users of coal globally are

a. China
b. United States
c. India
d. Canada
e. Russia

(A) A, B, and C
(B) A, B, and D
(C) B, D, and E
(D) A, B, and E

292. A lot of people tout natural gas as a "clean, natural" alternative to other fossil fuels. Which of the following is considered to be a benefit of using natural gas?

(A) It is more energy-efficient than coal.
(B) Natural gas has fewer harmful emissions when burned.
(C) Coal power plants are less expensive to build.
(D) Access to natural gas is easy.

293. Advocates of drilling for oil domestically believe that drilling in the Arctic National Wildlife Refuge (ANWR) in Alaska would decrease our dependence on foreign, imported oil. Opponents to drilling in ANWR feel

(A) drilling in ANWR would not harm the tundra, and it would rebound quickly
(B) there are not enough oil reserves to make it worth the ecological damage
(C) we should do more research before we drill there
(D) we should use more renewable energy so that this source would not be needed

294. Passive and active are two types of systems that use solar energy. Which of the following would be considered an active solar system?

(A) Use heavy blinds on windows to absorb sunlight.

(B) Plant a tree on the east side of a house to keep it cool.

(C) Use skylights to get more sunlight into the home.

(D) Install photovoltaic panels on the roof of your house.

295. Solar thermal systems use solar energy to generate high-temperature heat and electricity. What would be considered a disadvantage for this type of energy production?

(A) Net energy yield is low.

(B) Large tax breaks are available for these systems.

(C) They can be installed in unusable, arid land areas.

(D) The energy from the sun is free and abundant.

296. What is one disadvantage of using large-scale, solar-cell power plants?

(A) Energy can be transformed and stored during the night or cloudy days.

(B) These can be connected to wind farms for increased productivity.

(C) These can be installed on various hard surfaces, such as on the roofs of buildings and parking lots.

(D) Greenhouse gases are used to create the parts and materials needed.

297. One disadvantage to tapping dry- or wet-steam geothermal resources is that

(A) drilling that deeply runs the risk of provoking a volcanic eruption

(B) it is possible to deplete the heat in some underground reservoirs for a period of time

(C) releasing underground pressure can cause the overlying ground to sink, cracking buildings and streets

(D) drilling too close to a geologically active fault can increase the frequency of earthquakes

298. When Hoover Dam opened in 1936, it was the largest concrete structure in the world. Beginning in 1931, thousands of workers contributed to the project—more than 5,200 were working when the project was at its employment peak. Located at the border of Nevada and Arizona, Hoover Dam generates 2,080 megawatts for utilities in those two states and California. It's the single reason for the existence of the Lake Mead reservoir, which lies immediately upstream, and it controls flooding of the Colorado River below it.

(A) What sort of hydroelectric power plant is Hoover Dam? What is its power classification?

(B) Would electricity from Hoover Dam be fairly represented as renewable energy?

(C) What are Hoover Dam's negative environmental effects?

299. This energy source is the only one that is: renewable, independent of the sun, and has its ultimate source within the earth (in the form of heat in steam and hot water).

(A) geothermal energy

(B) wind power

(C) tidal energy

(D) solar energy

300. Which of the following is considered to be a disadvantage of using geothermal energy?

(A) high polluting emissions

(B) high initial capital costs

(C) wasteful by-products

(D) deep drilling and hard to access

301. Which country is the largest producer of geothermal energy in the world?

(A) Iceland

(B) India

(C) Indonesia

(D) United States

302. Which of the following has NOT been proposed as a method for storing hydrogen fuel?

(A) cooling it to liquid form

(B) compressing it as a gas

(C) absorbing it with metal hydride compounds

(D) cooling it to solid form

303. The uranium oxide pellets used in typical nuclear reactors are primarily composed of the nonfissionable isotope

(A) uranium-235

(B) uranium-238

(C) uranium-258

(D) uranium-255

304. Inside a reactor, a neutron strikes a uranium atom nucleus, which splits, releasing a great deal of energy and sending fragments of the nucleus speeding away in different directions. This single sequence of events is best described as an example of

(A) fusion

(B) fission

(C) enrichment

(D) meltdown

305. After operating for up to 60 years, conventional nuclear plants must be either renovated or decommissioned for which two main reasons?

  I. Many parts become radioactive.

 II. Spent fuel rods cannot be removed from the core.

III. Many parts become brittle or corroded.

IV. Pressure inside the core increases until it reaches the facility's limit.

(A) I and II

(B) II and III

(C) I and III

(D) II and IV

306. Radioactive materials are dangerous to organisms such as humans because

(A) they neutralize the electrical charges of biological molecules, rendering them inert

(B) cells will substitute radioactive elements for oxygen and suffocate

(C) they cause proteins to replicate themselves uncontrollably

(D) they release particles that ionize DNA molecules

307. A nuclear reactor that makes more fissionable fuel is specifically known as a

(A) fusion reactor

(B) tokamak reactor

(C) moderator reactor

(D) breeder reactor

308. Glen Canyon Dam in Page, Arizona, is the second largest dam on the Colorado River. There is opposition to this dam and the building of others by many environmental groups. China now has the world's largest dam, and it, too, is criticized for its environmental impact.

(A) Describe three benefits that dams provide to people.

(B) The city of Springfield has plans to build a new dam. Assume that you work for an environmental group that opposes the dam. Using the example of the Three Gorges Dam in China, write a letter to be mailed to the residents explaining why they should reject funding for this project in the next election.

(C) Identify and describe four ways that the water supply can be managed to avoid building a dam in the future.

309. When spent nuclear fuel rods are stored temporarily at a nuclear reactor, they are often put into pools of boron-treated water to prevent them from

(A) undergoing an uncontrollable chain reaction resulting in a nuclear explosion

(B) turning to difficult-to-manage radioactive dust after further decay

(C) spreading throughout the facility as they melt into liquid form

(D) heating up, catching fire, and releasing contaminants into the environment

310. The open nuclear fuel cycle does NOT involve

(A) reprocessing spent fuel into usable fissionable material

(B) burying radioactive wastes underground for thousands of years

(C) mining uranium-containing ore from the earth

(D) decommissioning old reactors

311. Hydrogen fuel cells are a very low polluting gas because when hydrogen gas burns in the air it combines with oxygen to create which by-product?

(A) carbon dioxide

(B) water vapor

(C) nitrous oxide

(D) ozone

312. Transuranium elements can be obtained only by

(A) mining deposits located deep under the ocean

(B) refining petroleum using high-pressure processes

(C) bombarding heavy elements with neutrons

(D) treating uranium ores with corrosive chemicals

313. Which of the following is NOT a drawback of nuclear energy?

(A) highly dangerous waste products
(B) potential for catastrophic plant accident
(C) high upfront investment in plant construction
(D) high air pollution from normal operations

314. Which three of the following are components of the open nuclear fuel cycle?

  I. decommissioning of old power plants
 II. mining uranium ore
III. generating electricity with a steam-driven turbine
IV. reprocessing of radioactive waste into fuel
 V. pumping of coolant through the core
VI. storage of high-level radioactive waste

(A) I, II, and III
(B) I, II, and VI
(C) II, III, and IV
(D) III, IV, and V

315. A disadvantage that nuclear energy has compared with coal is

(A) land disruption due to mining
(B) air pollution
(C) contribution to acid rain
(D) difficulty of plant construction and maintenance

316. Fusion reactors are NOT used for energy production because they

(A) produce dangerous amounts of radiation
(B) can explode with the force of a hydrogen bomb in an accident
(C) produce a large amount of high-level radioactive waste compared with fission reactors
(D) have not yet produced more energy from fuel than they consume

317. In 2003, the Paks Nuclear Power Plant near Paks, Hungary, experienced a serious incident that could have been much worse. While a special machine was being used to clean fuel rods at the bottom of a special water pool, inadequate water circulation allowed some rods to heat up, probably cracking them a little, and the pool's water began to register an increased level of radioactivity. When workers opened the cleaning device underwater, a sudden change in temperature damaged the rods' outside coating enough to allow uranium fuel pellets to spill into the bottom of the cleaning tank, with some of the elements piling together—a situation that caused inspectors to immediately raise their assessment of the incident's seriousness. Power plant workers poured boric acid into the water, and they eventually cleaned up the mess.

(A) Even if the rods had not released uranium pellets, what might have happened had the rods been allowed to heat up further?

(B) Why would inspectors find a pile of uranium pellets so concerning?

(C) Why would workers pour boric acid into the pool? What effect would it have?

318. Wafers of layered semiconductor sheets that produce electrical current when exposed to light are technically known as

(A) photovoltaic cells

(B) thermal cells

(C) visible spectrum cells

(D) passive solar cells

319. Dams that allow water to flow through at a controlled rate can generate electricity if the water turns a turbine on its way out. This kind of power plant produces

(A) dam power

(B) geothermal power

(C) kinetic power

(D) hydroelectric power

320. Which of the following is often a disadvantage of damming rivers to generate electricity?

(A) low-efficiency conversion of water kinetic energy to electricity

(B) short power-plant life, requiring frequent decommissioning

(C) negative environmental impact from flooding behind a dam and decreased silt flow below the dam

(D) high carbon dioxide emissions from electricity-generating equipment

321. One of the main problems with switching to ethanol as a fuel in the United States is that

(A) it takes a great deal of energy to produce ethanol from corn, the major crop used in its production

(B) automobile engines have not yet been developed to use ethanol

(C) ethanol cannot be made in a renewable way

(D) burning ethanol releases large amounts of sulfur into the atmosphere

322. Proposed methods for using geothermal energy include

(A) running turbines directly with hot gases expelled through volcanic vents

(B) channeling molten magma from live volcanoes to power plants to run steam turbines

(C) capturing hydrogen sulfide gas for use as a flammable fuel

(D) heating a home's water by piping it underground and back

323. Wind turbines can produce more power when they

(A) generate direct current rather than alternating current

(B) are constructed with longer blades

(C) are mounted higher off the ground

(D) have five or more blades each

324. All of the following are examples of wind power's disadvantages EXCEPT

(A) wind power can be inconsistent
(B) wind farms require a large amount of space
(C) wind turbines make noise
(D) wind turbines generate direct current that must be converted to alternating current

325. Wind energy is a growing energy source. Wind energy is captured by _____ and converted into _____.

(A) kinetic energy; electrical energy
(B) blades; potential energy
(C) potential energy; kinetic energy
(D) blades; electrical energy

326. Which country is the world leader in wind energy production?

(A) China
(B) Finland
(C) Sweden
(D) Germany

327. Which of the following is considered an advantage of using nuclear power plants to create electricity?

(A) Little to no air pollutants are produced.
(B) Decommissioning is expensive.
(C) Water pollution is high.
(D) Much carbon dioxide is released during processing.

328. Corporate average fuel economy (CAFE) standards are regulations in the United States set in place to improve the fuel economy of all the following vehicles EXCEPT

(A) small cars
(B) large cars
(C) semi-trailer trucks
(D) diesel trucks

329. According to corporate average fuel economy (CAFE) standards, as of 2017, the standard fuel economy for domestic passenger cars is more than _____ miles per gallon of gasoline.

(A) 38
(B) 45
(C) 55
(D) 65

330. If you run a 100-watt light bulb for 4 hours, how many kWh of energy did you use?

(A) 100 kWh
(B) 400 kWh
(C) 0.1 kWh
(D) 0.4 kWh

Atmospheric Pollution

331. Smog levels are usually highest in

(A) fall
(B) winter
(C) spring
(D) summer

332. Which of the following air pollutants are from an anthropogenic origin?

(A) radon
(B) ozone
(C) methane
(D) chlorofluorocarbons

333. In which atmospheric layer does air pollution affect humans the most?

(A) mesosphere
(B) stratosphere
(C) exosphere
(D) troposphere

334. On the night of December 2, 1984, an accident in a pesticide plant occurred that released a toxic chemical cloud that killed many people. Where did this event take place?

(A) Bhopal, India
(B) Three Mile Island, Pennsylvania
(C) Love Canal, New York
(D) Chernobyl, Ukraine

335. The Clean Air Act requires the Environmental Protection Agency (EPA) to set National Ambient Air Quality Standards (NAAQS) for maximum allowable concentrations of six "criteria" pollutants in outdoor air. These pollutants can harm human health and cause issues in the environment. According to the Clean Air Act, which of the following is listed as one of the six primary pollutants?

(A) stratospheric ozone
(B) nitrogen dioxide
(C) chlorofluorocarbons
(D) mercury

336. Under the Clean Air Act, EPA has established National Ambient Air Quality Standards (NAAQS) for the 6 Criteria Air Pollutants, which are carbon monoxide, lead, ground-level ozone, particulate matter, nitrogen dioxide, and

(A) mercury
(B) potassium
(C) sulfur dioxide
(D) soot

337. Fine particulate matter is an air pollutant that is a concern for people's health when levels are high. What size PM (particulate matter) is considered unhealthy or dangerous for human health?

(A) PM 100
(B) PM 25
(C) PM 10
(D) PM 2.5

338. This primary pollutant is a mixture of contaminants formed when nitrogen oxide and volatile organic compounds (VOCs) react to sunlight, creating a brown haze above cities.

(A) water vapor
(B) smoke particles
(C) ozone
(D) photochemical smog

339. What is the leading cause of photochemical smog?

(A) industrial smokestacks
(B) vehicle exhaust
(C) coal-fired power plants
(D) gasoline stations

340. At least two distinct types of smog are recognized as air pollution. One example is called photochemical smog, and the other is called "London smog." What is the main source of "London smog"?

(A) carbon dioxide from burning fossil fuels
(B) sulfur oxides from burning of fossil fuels
(C) methane from decomposition in landfills
(D) carbon monoxide from coal-burning power plants

341. Based on the pollution levels of major cities, where would you find the worst air pollution in the world?

(A) China
(B) Pakistan
(C) Mexico
(D) India

342. Historically, which U.S. city has the highest levels of photochemical smog?

(A) Chicago
(B) New York
(C) New Orleans
(D) Los Angeles

343. Normally, air temperature decreases with an increase in altitude. During this phenomenon, warmer air is held above cooler air and the standard temperature profile with altitude is inverted. This event will trap air pollution, such as smog, close to the ground.

(A) thermal smog cap
(B) thermal inversion
(C) thermal reversal
(D) thermal invasion

344. A thermal inversion will control AQI levels near the ground. A strong thermal inversion will trap pollutants, leading to high AQI levels. What does the term AQI stand for?

(A) air quality index
(B) air quality indicator
(C) air quantity interval
(D) air quality interval

345. One of the most famous examples of thermal inversion pollution in a city, lethal smog covered this city for five days, starting on December 5, 1952. The smog was caused by a combination of industrial pollution and high-pressure weather conditions that trapped the pollution. This combination of smoke and fog resulted in thousands of human deaths and other severe respiratory issues. In which city did this event take place?

(A) Chicago, USA
(B) Los Angeles, USA
(C) Bhopal, India
(D) London, England

346. The city in the United States distinguished by having the most stringent pollution control program and the most significant air pollution problem due to tropospheric ozone is

(A) Detroit
(B) Boston
(C) Denver
(D) Los Angeles/Long Beach

347. Much of the air in China is dangerously polluted with photochemical smog, especially in heavily populated cities such as Beijing that has a lot of vehicle exhaust. It is estimated in 2007 that approximately _____ Chinese died prematurely due to health issues associated with air pollution.

(A) 10,000
(B) 25,000
(C) 100,000
(D) 400,000

348. Carbon sequestration is the natural or artificial process of long-term storage of carbon dioxide. Which of the following is an example of carbon sequestration?

(A) formation of carbonate deposits in the oceans
(B) outgassing by volcanoes near the equator
(C) respiration by mammals on land
(D) respiration by anaerobic bacteria in the oceans

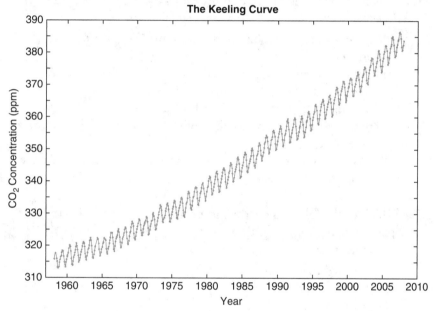

Figure 7.1

349. The graph in Figure 7.1 is referred to as the Keeling curve. Charles David Keeling was the first to begin measuring the amount of carbon dioxide (CO_2) in the atmosphere. He noticed that there were fluctuations in the CO_2 concentrations yearly, although the average yearly concentration continued to increase at a rapid pace. What did Charles David Keeling realize that the annual decreases in CO_2 correlated with?

(A) less air conditioning use in the winter
(B) more electricity use in the summer
(C) more photosynthesis in the fall/winter
(D) more photosynthesis in the spring/summer

350. One major solution for reducing the amount of carbon dioxide in the atmosphere is

(A) increase oceanic temperatures to increase phytoplankton growth
(B) increase the transition of tropical rainforests to agricultural land
(C) decrease the total area of aquatic agriculture (such as rice paddies)
(D) decrease the use of fossil fuels (such as coal, oil and natural gas)

351. Which of the following carbon reservoirs have the longest residence time?

(A) carbon stored as wood after photosynthesis, then used as firewood that winter
(B) carbon stored as maple sugar in a tree, then used as fuel for cellular respiration by animals that eat it
(C) carbon incorporated into a carbonate shell that falls to the bottom of the ocean as sediment, then forms a rock (such as limestone)
(D) carbon from peat bogs harvested and used in garden beds five years after they were deposited

352. Which of the following is the most significant contributor to PM (particulate matter) pollution?

(A) hybrid vehicle exhaust
(B) unpaved roads and fields
(C) dust storms
(D) power plants

353. When looking at climate data, scientists can use indirect proxy data for atmospheric carbon dioxide concentrations in the past. Which process can read meteorological climate data from over 800,000 years in the past?

(A) fossil evidence
(B) ice cores
(C) tree rings
(D) pollen data

354. This indoor air pollutant can cause dizziness, headaches, confusion, nausea, and even death. It is caused by incomplete combustion of fossil fuels and can build up indoors. It is especially deadly because human blood hemoglobin has an affinity for this gas, which causes internal suffocation due to the lack of oxygen to the vital organs.

(A) ozone
(B) carbon monoxide
(C) carbon dioxide
(D) sulfur dioxide

355. This indoor air pollutant is a radioactive gas that forms naturally when radioactive metals break down in rocks, soil, and groundwater that is often found in basements of homes built on bedrock.

(A) carbon monoxide
(B) radon
(C) photochemical smog
(D) ozone

356. Indoor air quality can be affected by unclean air conditioning ducts. People can become seriously ill if a building's air circulation is not maintained properly. People can get "Pontiac fever" when they breathe in small droplets of water in the air that contain bacteria. What is another name for this air pollution disease?

(A) Legionnaires' disease
(B) Pontiac's disease
(C) Hashimoto's disease
(D) anthrax

357. This is a naturally occurring fibrous mineral that can cause lung cancer when small pieces become airborne and inhaled. It has been used in a wide variety of construction materials for insulation and as a fire retardant because of its fiber strength and resistance to heat.

(A) formaldehyde
(B) asbestos
(C) chlorine
(D) soot

358. One important naturally occurring indoor air pollutant is radon. radon comes from the breakdown of a radioactive element found in soils and rocks. What is radon a by-product of?

(A) selenium
(B) uranium
(C) radium
(D) potassium

359. What is the name of the international treaty signed in 1997 by the United Nations to reduce the amount of greenhouse gases released into the atmosphere that contributes to global climate change?

(A) the Paris Treaty
(B) Kyoto Protocol
(C) Montreal Protocol
(D) the Paris Accord

360. In what year was the Clean Air Act established in the United States?

(A) 1952
(B) 1960
(C) 1963
(D) 1975

361. Which major electricity generating source has a low environmental impact, is high performance, releases no greenhouse gas emissions, and can supply power at any time (day or night)?

(A) solar array
(B) wind turbines
(C) nuclear energy
(D) natural gas

362. This air pollution reduction device that uses charged metal plates to remove particulates from smokestack emissions.

(A) dry scrubber
(B) electrostatic precipitator
(C) lime cleaner
(D) electromagnetic smoke collector

363. In this air pollution deduction method, the polluted gas stream is brought into contact with a specialized solution—typically by spraying it with the liquid or forcing it through a pool of liquid—so as to remove the pollutants from the emissions.

(A) electromagnetic smoke collector
(B) electrostatic precipitator
(C) lime cleaner
(D) wet scrubber

364. "Normal" rainwater is naturally acidic, with a pH of about 5.6. Natural variations and human pollutants may cause rain to be more or less acidic. The natural acidity of rainwater is attributed to this compound

(A) VOCs
(B) nitrogen dioxide
(C) ozone
(D) carbonic acid

365. Acid deposition (acid rain) is defined as precipitation that falls in wet or dry forms that has a pH that is lower than usual. Where is "acid rain" most commonly found?

(A) downwind of a coal-fired power plant
(B) upwind of an industrial plant
(C) in the soil around a smokestack
(D) near excessive fertilizer and pesticide use

366. Acidity and alkalinity are measured using a pH scale for which 7.0 is neutral. Regular rainfall has a pH of about 5.6. Acid rain usually has a pH between 4.2 and 4.6. If acid rain has a pH of 4.6, how much more acidic is it than "normal" rain?

(A) 1×
(B) 2×
(C) 10×
(D) 100×

Use the following graph in Figure 7.2 for Questions 367–369.

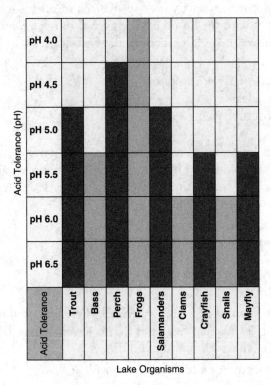

Figure 7.2

367. Use the preceding chart for the species found in a local lake to determine which species would be the most tolerant to changes in pH due to acid rain.

(A) trout and bass
(B) clams and snails
(C) frogs
(D) mayflies

368. Using the chart above for the species found in a local lake, which species would be the best indicator species for changes in the pH of the lake?

(A) trout and bass
(B) clams and snails
(C) frogs
(D) salamanders

369. In the chart above for the species found in a local lake, perch has a pH range of 6.5 to 4.5. What is the difference in pH value between 6.5 and 4.5?

(A) 1×
(B) 2×
(C) 10×
(D) 100×

370. Rainwater mixes with which of the following to form carbonic acid?

(A) hydrochloric acid
(B) carbon dioxide
(C) carbon monoxide
(D) sulfur dioxide

371. Acid rain affects trees by

   I. damaging the protective coating on leaves
  II. leaching nutrients from the soil and away from trees
 III. stunting growth

(A) I only
(B) II only
(C) I and II only
(D) I, II, and III

372. Many animals use sound to find food, shelter, and mates. They can also use sound to communicate with others or navigate. Environmental noise pollution can cause them harm by interfering with how they utilize sound. The study of the effects of noise pollution is referred to as

(A) echomation
(B) echolocation
(C) bioacoustics
(D) biolocation

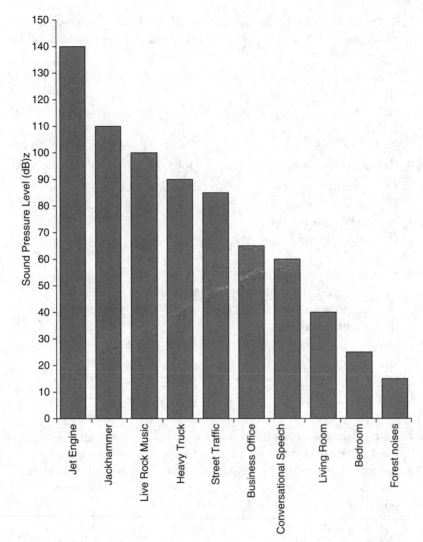

Figure 7.3

373. Figure 7.3 is a chart that ranks different sounds in terms of decibels (dB). In general, sounds above _____ are considered harmful to human ears and can contribute to hearing loss.

(A) 60 dB
(B) 75 dB
(C) 85 dB
(D) 100 dB

374. Which of these scenarios can be contributed to the effects of noise pollution?
    (A) more predation and animal attacks
    (B) whales beaching
    (C) animals flocking toward a particular source of noise
    (D) more biodiversity in an area

375. Noise pollution is measured in what units?
    (A) hertz (Hz)
    (B) milligrams (mg)
    (C) centimeters (cm)
    (D) decibels (dB)

Aquatic and Terrestrial Pollution

376. Of the following human activities, which two add sulfur dioxide to the environment?
  I. burning fossil fuels
  II. smelting ores to obtain metals
  III. disposing of radioactive waste
  IV. releasing fertilizer into rivers

  (A) I and II
  (B) II and III
  (C) III and IV
  (D) II and IV

377. Burning of fossil fuels directly affects which of the following?

  (A) insects eating plants
  (B) the nitrogen cycle
  (C) bird populations
  (D) increased nitrogen in plants

378. Municipal water pollution primarily comes from

  (A) chemical pesticides
  (B) oil operations
  (C) wastewater
  (D) fertilizers

379. Red tide blooms are caused by

(A) cryptosporidium
(B) dead zones
(C) El Niño
(D) storm runoff

380. Nonpoint source contamination of water includes all of the following EXCEPT

(A) rainfall
(B) pesticide residues in soil
(C) water from waste treatment plants
(D) emissions from automobiles

381. Which nutrient becomes a pollutant and is found in detergents and fertilizer?

(A) nitrogen
(B) phosphorus
(C) hazardous waste
(D) pathogens

382. Power plants, industry, mining, and medical tracers are all sources of what type of pollution?

(A) pathogens
(B) oil spills
(C) radioactive waste
(D) thermal pollution

383. Chlorofluorocarbons are pollutants because they

(A) turn lakes acidic
(B) break down the ozone layer
(C) contribute to global warming
(D) both B and C

384. Which by-product of manufacturing is slowly released from sediments into water and is biomagnified in the food chain, causing numerous health problems?

(A) sodium
(B) nitrates
(C) chlorine
(D) methyl mercury

385. Volcanoes, fossil fuel combustion, and fires contribute to pollution in the form of

(A) synthetic compounds
(B) DDT
(C) EMFs
(D) particulates

386. Carbon monoxides, VOCs, hydrocarbons, nitrogen oxides, peroxyacetyl nitrate, benzene, and lead are all pollutants produced by

(A) indoor air pollution
(B) gasoline-powered vehicles
(C) mining
(D) manufacturing

387. Excess nutrients in waterways can cause widespread ecological damage. The nutrients can cause algal blooms, which in turn will die off and increase oxygen demand in the water from the decomposers. This results in what is called a dead zone. The hypoxic "dead zone" fed by the Mississippi River is primarily a result of

(A) the river delivering too much sediment into the Gulf of Mexico
(B) sediment runoff from construction sites into the Gulf of Mexico
(C) lack of freshwater flow into the Gulf of Mexico
(D) runoff that contains nitrates from agricultural fields and sewage treatment plants

388. Which law sets the standard for the level of key water pollutants and requires polluters to obtain permits that limit how much of the various pollutants can be discharged into aquatic systems?

(A) Water Pollution Control Act of 1972
(B) Coastal Zone Water Control Act of 1980
(C) Water Quality and Pollution Act of 1987
(D) Clean Water Act of 1977

389. Which of the following would be an example of cultural eutrophication?

(A) excess sediment load due to erosion of the riverbank in heavy rains
(B) decrease in vegetation due to low dissolved oxygen levels in the water
(C) runoff from an agricultural area with heavy farming and fertilizer use
(D) excess sediment load due to weathering of sandstone due to high winds

390. Waterways near areas with high human population densities can experience large algal blooms or increases in other unwanted bacteria growth, often due to a lack of secondary waste treatment facilities. This is a result of

(A) rainwater runoff from storm drains
(B) sediment runoff from construction sites
(C) overfertilization of lawns and gardens
(D) large nutrient flows from sewage treatment plants

391. If an industry uses natural gas for manufacturing and then uses the waste heat for electricity production, this process would be referred to as

(A) cogeneration
(B) energy reclamation
(C) gas hydration
(D) gasification

392. Thermal pollution is defined as a sudden change in the temperature of a natural body of water caused by human activities. What effect would an increase in water temperature cause to a small lake?

(A) increase biodiversity due to more food availability
(B) decrease in water evaporation
(C) increase in carbon dioxide
(D) decrease in dissolved oxygen

393. What is the greatest source of anthropogenic thermal pollution in waterways?

(A) wave action
(B) effluent from power plants
(C) landfills
(D) agricultural waste

394. Persistent organic pollutants (POPs) such as DDT and PCB are dangerous to human health and the health of the environment because they

(A) remain in the environment, bioaccumulate, and biomagnify throughout the food chain
(B) are radioactive and carcinogenic substances
(C) are corrosive
(D) contribute to an increase in greenhouse gases

395. Persistent organic pollutants such as DDT are very harmful to wildlife when they are exposed to them, either acutely or chronically. Exposure to DDT is especially harmful to large predatory birds, such as the bald eagle, because DDT

(A) is a neurotoxin
(B) causes respiratory infections
(C) kills all of the prey species
(D) softens the eggshells of the birds so that they become crushed

396. How do POPs (persistent organic pollutants) such as DDT get ingested by the largest predatory animals?

(A) It bioaccumulates and biomagnifies up the food chain from the smallest organisms.

(B) It is sprayed directly on bird nests.

(C) It is fed to the small fish as a pesticide.

(D) It is dumped into the ocean to kill off pest species.

397. Spraying DDT for mosquito control in a local waterway will cause DDT to accumulate in the cells of microscopic aquatic organisms. After feeding on these organisms, filter feeders like clams (as well as some fish) ingest the DDT. If the microscopic aquatic organisms have 0.06 ppm of DDT in their bodies, what is the concentration on the next level of the food chain?

(A) 0.0006 ppm

(B) 0.006 ppm

(C) 0.06 ppm

(D) 0.6 ppm

398. Bioaccumulation is the buildup of harmful substances, such as pesticides or other chemicals, in an organism. Which of the following disasters associated with the following locations would be considered an example of bioaccumulation in a human food chain?

(A) Bhopal, India

(B) Valdez, Alaska

(C) Minamata, Japan

(D) Love Canal, New York

399. Which of the following would be most affected by the process of biomagnification?

(A) sardines

(B) zooplankton

(C) seagull

(D) phytoplankton

400. When building a sanitary landfill, engineers must include pipes that pump out the wastewater that seeps through the landfill over time. This contaminated water is referred to as

(A) primary pollutants
(B) leachate
(C) soot
(D) sewage

401. Many environmental scientists advocate that the best and least expensive way to deal with solid waste issues is to

(A) incinerate it to create electricity
(B) bury it in landfills
(C) dump in the ocean trenches
(D) reduce waste before it is produced

402. According to the U.S. Environmental Protection Agency, this material accounts for more than 40% of a landfill's content and is the most frequently encountered item in landfills.

(A) paper
(B) plastic
(C) water
(D) wood

403. This by-product of decomposition is created in landfills and needs to be pumped out to avoid any hazards. It also can be used as a resource in energy generation.

(A) propane
(B) butane
(C) carbon dioxide
(D) methane

404. Water flows slowly through grit chambers, allowing sand and small particles to settle out during which phase of water treatment?

(A) primary treatment
(B) secondary treatment
(C) tertiary treatment
(D) flocculation

405. This process in wastewater treatment uses aeration and bacteria to help to biologically break down the waste.

(A) activated sludge
(B) aeration and condensation
(C) biological activation
(D) biological consumption

406. In the United States, mass production of which of the following alternative energy sources could cause an increase in food prices?

(A) geothermal
(B) wind
(C) ethanol
(D) solar

407. An herbicide was used to kill some weeds. The label has the LD50 listed for rats at 250 mg/kg. What is the LD50?

(A) 50% of any rat population exposed to the herbicide will get sick.
(B) 500 of 1,000 warm-blooded mammals will die when they ingest the herbicide.
(C) 500 of 1,000 rats will die when they ingest the pesticide.
(D) 50% of a human population is likely to die when eating the pesticide-covered food.

408. A plot of data showing the effects of various doses of a toxic agent on a group of test organisms is called a

(A) lethal dose curve
(B) effective dose curve
(C) LD50 curve
(D) dose-response curve

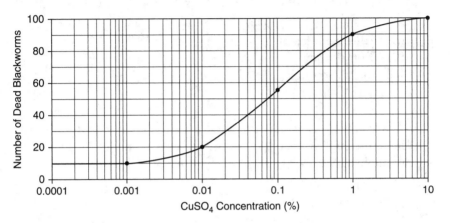

Figure 8.1

409. Approximately what is the value of the LD50 of $CuSO_4$ in the Figure 8.1?

(A) 0.001%
(B) 0.01%
(C) 0.1%
(D) 1%

410. Which of the following common diseases is transmitted through unsafe, contaminated drinking water?

(A) swine flu
(B) COVID-19
(C) cholera
(D) malaria

411. The main method of water disinfection in major cities is

    (A) ozone oxidation
    (B) ultraviolet light
    (C) turbidity
    (D) chlorination

412. Which of the following choices was once a potential solution for the long-term storage of high-level radioactive waste from nuclear power generation?

    (A) Minamata, Japan
    (B) Bhopal, India
    (C) Yucca Mountain, Nevada
    (D) Love Canal, New York

413. Which waste management method reduces the most waste volume but emits high levels of toxins into the environment and is harmful to human health?

    (A) sanitary landfill
    (B) ocean dumping
    (C) plastic recycling
    (D) waste incineration

414. Lead poisoning is particularly severe because it causes so many serious health problems, especially in children. This problem seems to occur at a higher incidence rate in African-American households at lower socioeconomic levels.

    (A) Why does this pollutant disproportionately affect those in poverty?
    (B) What are some ways to prevent lead poisoning?
    (C) How are people in nonindustrialized countries exposed to lead, and how are they affected by it?

415. Not all chemicals are equal when it comes to being dangerous. For a decision if something is a pollutant to the environment, both the chemical itself and the amount must be considered to determine the threat to human and environmental health.

(A) Distinguish between the LD_{50} and TD_{50} of a pollutant.

(B) Explain why the Clean Water Act may have no threshold for a pollutant.

(C) Discuss an ecological gradient near a smokestack that emits sulfur dioxide in high quantities.

416. A coliform test is used to detect which substance in water sources?

(A) dissolved oxygen

(B) mercury

(C) human or animal waste (feces)

(D) nitrates

417. Waterborne illnesses can cause a variety of symptoms. These can include skin, ear, respiratory, eye problems, diarrhea, and vomiting. Which one of these diseases are considered to be "waterborne"?

(A) flu

(B) giardiasis

(C) COVID-19

(D) malaria

418. Which one of these pest vectors can transmit Lyme disease to humans and animals?

(A) ticks

(B) mosquitos

(C) salmonella (bacteria)

(D) leeches

419. Which of these organisms can contribute to the malaria epidemic worldwide?

(A) ticks

(B) mosquitos

(C) salmonella

(D) leeches

420. Why does climate change contribute to the increase of disease-causing vectors in some areas of the world?

    (A) Less rain causes more mosquitos.

    (B) More rain will contribute to more mosquitos.

    (C) Warming will cause less biodiversity.

    (D) Warming will cause species to perish in higher latitudes.

CHAPTER 9

Global Change

421. The ozone layer in the stratosphere is very important to life on earth, particularly organisms on land. It filters ultraviolet radiation from the sun, protecting organisms and keeping the temperature on earth at a tolerable level. Ozone in the troposphere is classified as a pollutant. It can adversely affect the health of humans and other organisms.

    (A) What is the function of the ozone layer in the stratosphere?

    (B) What chemical reactions play a part in the degradation of the ozone layer in the stratosphere?

    (C) What is the source of the ozone in the troposphere? What health problems can it cause?

422. The ozone layer absorbs

    (A) infrared radiation from the sun

    (B) ultraviolet radiation from the sun

    (C) positively charged ions

    (D) heat radiated off earth's surface

423. Which of these does NOT have a natural source?

    (A) carbon dioxide

    (B) CFCs

    (C) nitrous oxide

    (D) vapor

424. What process do CFCs, chlorine, and bromine have in common that leads to destruction of the ozone layer?

(A) polymerization
(B) deposition
(C) photodissociation
(D) buffering

425. The breakdown of the ozone layer is dangerous because a thin ozone layer absorbs less

(A) UV radiation
(B) CFCs
(C) acid rain
(D) water vapor

426. In which season does the Antarctic ozone hole decrease by over 50% annually?

(A) Antarctic summer
(B) Antarctic fall
(C) Antarctic winter
(D) Antarctic spring

427. The stratospheric ozone layer is crucial to protect living things on earth. It is a natural layer of gas located in the upper atmosphere that protects humans and other living things from

(A) infrared radiation
(B) the visible light spectrum
(C) gamma radiation
(D) ultraviolet radiation

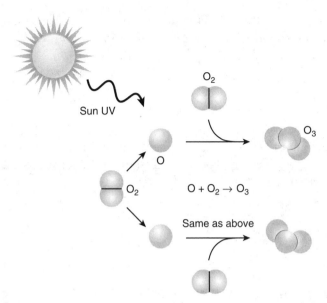

Figure 9.1

428. According to the diagram in Figure 9.1, what causes the oxygen molecule to break apart in the formation of ozone?

(A) chlorofluorocarbons
(B) DDT
(C) ultraviolet light
(D) O_2

429. One pollution control measure in which companies can sell "credits" for emissions is known as

(A) deposition credits
(B) tradable license
(C) deposition permits
(D) tradable permits

430. The Montreal Protocol, finalized in 1987, is a global agreement to do what?

(A) reduce the use and release of chlorofluorocarbons into the atmosphere
(B) help reduce acid rain by decreasing carbon dioxide emissions
(C) strengthen laws to stop the trade in endangered species
(D) reduce carbon dioxide emissions by increasing the development of alternative energy sources

431. Chlorofluorocarbons (CFCs) are the main cause of anthropogenic ozone depletion. What are CFCs used for?

(A) plastics
(B) paper products
(C) water softeners
(D) refrigerants and propellants

432. Depletion of the protective ozone layer can increase our exposure to _____. This can harm humans, other life forms, and materials. Excess exposure may lead to skin cancer.

(A) UV-A
(B) UV-B
(C) UV-C
(D) UV-D

433. If humans comply with the Montreal Protocol and discontinue the use of ODC (ozone-depleting compounds), the ozone layer is predicted to be fully repaired by

(A) 2020
(B) 2030
(C) 2040
(D) 2050

434. Chlorofluorocarbons are harmful and break apart ozone. Where are they most damaging in the atmosphere?

(A) ionosphere
(B) stratosphere
(C) thermosphere
(D) exosphere

435. Nitrogen oxides make up what percentage of U.S. emissions of greenhouse gases?

(A) 35%
(B) 14%
(C) 60%
(D) 72%

436. How much higher is the amount of carbon dioxide in the atmosphere today compared to the mid-1700s?

(A) 80%

(B) 50%

(C) 145%

(D) 30%

437. Approximately how much of the sunlight reaching earth is reflected back into space?

(A) ¾

(B) ½

(C) ⅓

(D) ⅛

438. Deforestation, burning of fossil fuels, and other activities that release greenhouse gases all contribute to

(A) solar emissions

(B) changing ocean currents

(C) decreasing sea levels

(D) global warming

439. Which of the following is NOT a source of methane?

(A) cows

(B) landfills

(C) forest fires

(D) aerosols

440. Rising sea levels that result from global warming are caused by

  I. melting of glaciers

 II. expanding oceans due to warmer temperatures

III. more rainfall

(A) I only

(B) II only

(C) I and II only

(D) II and III only

441. El Niño contributes to a temporary increase in global temperatures because it

(A) increases solar radiation
(B) increases deforestation
(C) causes rising sea levels
(D) increases heat in the atmosphere from warm ocean waters

442. Which type of organisms would thrive in global warming conditions?

(A) small mammals
(B) butterflies
(C) migratory birds
(D) infectious insects

443. Healthy oceans and forests

(A) are a carbon dioxide source
(B) are a carbon dioxide sink
(C) are an example of positive feedback
(D) contribute most of the greenhouse gases

444. Climate refers to

(A) conditions in the atmosphere that occur for weeks at a time in an area
(B) conditions in the atmosphere that occur for years at a time in an area
(C) the weather in the thermosphere
(D) the chemical elements in the atmosphere

445. The levels of carbon dioxide throughout the history of the earth can best be measured using

(A) ice cores
(B) fossils
(C) historical records
(D) snow

446. When energy from the sun gets absorbed by the ocean instead of being reflected by ice, this is known as

(A) El Niño
(B) polar amplification
(C) anthropogenic forcing
(D) solar radiation

447. The amount of carbon dioxide that was in the atmosphere hundreds of years ago can be measured using

(A) fossils
(B) air samples
(C) ocean samples
(D) glacial ice cores

448. Which of the following greenhouse gases is a by-product of anaerobic decomposition?

(A) methane
(B) ozone
(C) chlorofluorocarbons
(D) carbon monoxide

449. Greenhouse gases contribute to the increase in global temperatures. Which one of these gases is considered to be the most significant contributor to atmospheric warming?

(A) water vapor
(B) CH_4
(C) N_2O
(D) CO_2

450. Which of the following greenhouse gases has the most significant impact on the warming of earth's atmosphere?

(A) water vapor
(B) CFCs
(C) methane (CH_4)
(D) nitrogen dioxide (NO_2)

451. Which of the following greenhouse gases has the shortest residence time in the atmosphere?

(A) nitrogen dioxide (NO_x)
(B) CO_2
(C) CFCs
(D) methane (CH_4)

452. Which of the following is the most significant contributor to worldwide greenhouse gas emissions?

(A) China
(B) United States
(C) Russia
(D) Saudi Arabia

453. Which of the following greenhouse gases is produced only by anthropogenic means?

(A) CH_4
(B) O_3
(C) H_2O
(D) CFCs

454. Which greenhouse gas is correctly paired with its source?

(A) $NO_x \rightarrow$ photosynthesis
(B) methane $\rightarrow$ foam insulation
(C) carbon dioxide $\rightarrow$ burning fossil fuels
(D) CFCs $\rightarrow$ fire extinguishers

455. Which planet (other than earth) is known to have a "runaway greenhouse effect" due to excess greenhouse gases in the atmosphere?

(A) Mercury
(B) Mars
(C) Venus
(D) Jupiter

456. Which of the following is a possible outcome of increased global temperatures due to the greenhouse effect and climate change?

(A) flooding

(B) droughts in agricultural areas

(C) increased precipitation and surface runoff

(D) all of the above

457. Sea-level rise is one of the consequences of global warming. Sea-level rise is mostly caused by

(A) increased runoff into the oceans

(B) increased soil erosion into the oceans

(C) thermal expansion of water in the oceans due to rising temperatures

(D) increased cloud cover over land, increasing rain

458. Paleoclimatologists gather proxy data from natural recorders of climate variability. Which one of the following sources of climate data is a proxy source that records the longest amount of time?

(A) tree rings

(B) ice cores

(C) pollen records

(D) volcanic eruptions

459. Which of the following is the cause of natural, long-term changes in climate and are not associated with human activity?

(A) Milankovitch cycles

(B) the industrial revolution and burning of fossil fuels

(C) deforestation

(D) clear-cutting and increased agriculture

460. The El Niño–Southern Oscillation (ENSO) is a recurring climatic pattern that starts with ocean surface cooling or warming of waters in the central and eastern tropical Pacific Ocean. This change in ocean surface temperatures causes drastic changes to the climate of regions around the world. Which of the following events is caused by El Niño?

(A) increased rainfall to parts of Pacific Coast of South America
(B) cooler temperatures over Western and Central Canada
(C) wetter conditions in the Pacific Northwest
(D) stronger winds worldwide

461. Each year, carbon dioxide levels in the atmosphere reach a peak level around the same time in the winter. Globally, what is happening annually that would account for such a predictable repeating pattern of these increases in carbon dioxide?

(A) more coal-fired stoves in winter
(B) more cars on the road
(C) earth is closest to the sun
(D) winter in the Northern Hemisphere

462. Many environmentalists believe that eating less red meat will help to combat climate change. CAFOs (concentrated agricultural feeding operations) such as large-scale cattle farms contribute to climate change because

(A) the cattle release large amounts of methane, which is a greenhouse gas
(B) the cattle eat a lot of grass, which decreases the amount of CO_2 absorbed by grass
(C) the cattle waste (urine and feces) ends up in runoff in the ocean
(D) more plants equal more photosynthesis and less CO_2

463. Of the following alternative energy sources, which has the highest energy return on energy invested?

(A) photovoltaic solar
(B) hydroelectric
(C) geothermal
(D) wind

464. Which is the greatest threat to global sea-level rising?

(A) melting of the Antarctic ice shelf
(B) thermal expansion of the water
(C) breakdown of the polar ice caps
(D) increased erosion and river runoff

465. Which of the following would be a result of ocean warming?

(A) increase in hypoxia zones (low oxygen levels)
(B) decrease evaporation over the oceans
(C) decrease frequency and severity of storms (hurricanes)
(D) increase the pH of ocean water

466. Hypoxic zones can occur naturally. These are areas in which dissolved oxygen levels become dangerously low, and organisms start to die off in large quantities. Some of the causes are excess nutrients in the water and ocean warming. What is another name for these areas?

(A) low oxygen zones
(B) oxygen minimum areas
(C) oxygen missing zones
(D) dead zones

467. Which scenario would "hold" the most dissolved oxygen?

(A) salty and cold water
(B) fresh and cold water
(C) fresh and warm water
(D) salty and warm water

468. Increased ocean acidification will affect humans as well as ocean ecosystems. Ocean acidification will affect the food we eat since most of our shellfish require this compound to form or to fortify the shells they use for locomotion, protection, and their homes.

(A) carbon dioxide
(B) magnesium oxide
(C) calcium hydroxide
(D) calcium carbonate

469. The following is the first step in acidifying the oceans. First, CO_2 reacts with water to form _____ ($H_2CO_3^-$): Equation: $CO_2 + H_2O$ $H_2CO_3^-$.

Which compound is created when carbon dioxide and water are combined?

(A) carbon trioxide
(B) carbonate ions
(C) carbon dioxide water
(D) carbonic acid

470. Which substance acts as a buffer to help regulate the pH of seawater?

(A) carbon dioxide
(B) carbonate ions
(C) calcium carbonate
(D) carbonic acid

471. When the temperature or salinity of seawater decreases, the amount of carbon dioxide that can be absorbed will

(A) increase
(B) decrease
(C) remain the same
(D) depend on the organisms

472. The numerical value of pH is determined by the molar concentration of which ion?

(A) carbonate
(B) hydrogen
(C) hydroxide
(D) oxide

473. What is the approximate pH of typical ocean water?

(A) 6.5
(B) 7.5
(C) 8.1
(D) 8.9

474. Which ocean habitat is most affected by ocean acidification?

(A) coral reefs
(B) kelp forests
(C) deep ocean
(D) intertidal zones

475. This invasive species was released into Australia in 1935 to control the destructive cane beetle population that was decimating the cane sugar crops. They did not control the beetles but instead reproduced at an alarming rate and endangered many native species.

(A) cane grub
(B) cane toad
(C) Asian tiger mosquito
(D) Asian carp

476. Two countries are the most significant sources of invasive species worldwide due to the high level of trade connected to both of these countries and the high number of invasive species already found there.

(A) Mexico and Malaysia
(B) China and United States
(C) China and Canada
(D) China and Mexico

477. What is the term for a species that is native and restricted to a specific area?

(A) invasive

(B) non-native

(C) endemic

(D) epidemic

478. What is the difference between an alien and an invasive species?

(A) Invasive species are not harmful.

(B) Invasive species are venomous.

(C) Invasive species are aliens that cause significant harm.

(D) Aliens are from a nearby habitat.

479. When a forest is destroyed for lumber, the loss of revenue from tourists NOT visiting that area is known as a(n)

(A) risk value

(B) cost mitigation

(C) marginal cost

(D) externality

480. What percentage of the world's carbon dioxide comes from the United States?

(A) 90%

(B) 5%

(C) 20%

(D) 60%

481. The majority of wood in forests of developing countries is used for

(A) timber for construction

(B) firewood

(C) paper

(D) furniture

482. Each of the following might be part of an ecological restoration project EXCEPT

(A) replanting a forest in a heavily logged area
(B) removing a dam to allow a river to run naturally
(C) reintroducing native species to a grassland
(D) creating a wetland in a ruined grassland

483. Which South American country devotes a greater share of its land to biodiversity protection than any other country in the world?

(A) Brazil
(B) Costa Rica
(C) Nicaragua
(D) Venezuela

484. Which U.S. act forbids killing marine mammals or the selling/import of their body parts?

(A) Endangered Species Act
(B) Marine Mammal Protection Act
(C) Oceans Protection Act
(D) Invasive Species Act

485. Which of the following is why a species would become particularly vulnerable to extinction?

(A) high reproduction rate
(B) specialized feeding habits
(C) small size
(D) diversified habitat

486. Humans can increase an area's biodiversity when they

(A) drain a swamp to build a tree farm
(B) plow a field to plant crops
(C) break one large habitat into two smaller ones
(D) allow two populations of a species to trade members

487. Illegal hunting of endangered, protected animals in Africa. The meat is either eaten by the hunter or sold to earn needed income.

(A) endangered species trade
(B) bushmeat trade
(C) wild animal trade
(D) Africa meat trade

488. This deadly disease can be transmitted to humans from contact with contaminated meat and eating endangered bushmeat.

(A) malaria
(B) Ebola
(C) West Nile virus
(D) COVID-19

489. Biologists focus on biodiversity hot spots when concentrating their resources and research regarding biodiversity. Where are most of the biodiversity hot spots found on earth?

(A) grasslands
(B) deserts
(C) tropical rainforests
(D) tundra

490. When protecting biodiversity worldwide, what is the disadvantage of preserving a single large area?

(A) A natural disaster could destroy it all at once.
(B) There is less room for large species.
(C) There is more room for larger species, such as elephants.
(D) Resources could be focused on that area.

491. Roads, fences, and other human-produced barriers prevent some species from migrating as their environment changes. Cars are dangerous for road crossings, and the wide-open land from development can make animals more visible to predators. What is the term for an area of habitat that allows wildlife populations that are separated to be able to connect safely?

(A) animal byway
(B) land-use corridor
(C) habitat corridor
(D) habitat connector

492. This is the actual process of splitting up and separating natural habitat areas, causing animals to lose both their natural habitat and their ability to move between regions all due to human encroachment.

(A) habitat fragmentation
(B) habitat dividing
(C) island biodiversity
(D) habitat loss

493. Biodiversity also provides humans benefits in the form of monetary revenue. The pharmaceutical industry uses products derived from the third-world plants, animals, and microbes that brings an estimated _____ annually.

(A) $10 million
(B) $20 billion
(C) $30 billion
(D) $3 trillion

494. A volcanic eruption wiped out the vast majority of a species of small rodents that lived on the side of a mountain. A tiny population was able to survive and reproduce, but their offspring have different allele frequencies than those of the original larger population. Which of the following processes occurred in this scenario?

(A) evolution by gene flow
(B) evolution by the bottleneck effect
(C) evolution by the founder effect
(D) evolution by artificial selection

495. More than _____% of all of the species that have ever existed are now extinct.

(A) 10
(B) 25
(C) 75
(D) 99

496. Which of the following represents an ecosystem with high species abundance but low species diversity?

(A) a large monoculture field of corn
(B) an island with birds and insects
(C) an open field with grasses and wildflowers
(D) an old-growth forest

497. The major factors causing a decrease in biodiversity can be abbreviated with the acronym HIPPCO. One "P" is population growth. What does the other "P" stand for?

(A) population size
(B) pollution
(C) poaching
(D) pricing

498. Which of the following is an example of overexploitation of species?

(A) eutrophication
(B) dead zones
(C) ocean acidification
(D) overfishing

499. This marine protected area is the largest conservation area in the United States, and also one of the largest marine conservation areas in the world.

(A) Channel Islands National Park
(B) Papahānaumokuākea Marine National Monument
(C) Everglades National Park
(D) Great Lakes

500. Farmers and breeders have always used this process to cause significant changes in their plants and animals' characteristics over time. They have manipulated the plants and animals with desirable traits to reproduce, causing the evolution of farm products. This type of selective breeding is referred to as

(A) artificial selection
(B) selective pressures
(C) selective diversity
(D) selective cropping

ANSWERS

Chapter 1: Living World: Ecosystems

21. (A) The cave ecosystem ultimately depends upon producers in the outside world—plants that photosynthesize using sunlight and are eaten by consumers (or a series of consumers) that die or leave droppings in caves. However, the lowest level of the cave food chain is the decomposer fungi and bacteria, which serve an underground role that is similar to the role of producers.

(B) Primary consumers in the caves are those creatures that eat bacteria and fungi, such as millipedes and flatworms.

(C) The secondary consumers in this example are spiders and salamanders.

22. (A) A temperate rain forest has conifer trees, large amounts of rainfall, and cool temperatures. This is found only in a few small regions of the world.

23. (C) A niche is the role or function that an organism plays in the environment.

24. (D) The other four components are essential to any ecosystem.

25. (A) Nitrogen, in the form of nitrates or ammonia, is a component of of proteins that are used to make enzymes and other compounds to help the plant live.

26. (D) The highest predators are the most dependent upon a stable ecosystem.

27. (B) Physical damage does not affect the niche where its species survives and interacts with its ecosystem.

28. (D) The composition of the earth's core is metallic, primarily iron and nickel, and it does not generally exchange material with the mantle.

29. (D) The lysocline is the ocean depth below which higher pressure allows more carbon dioxide to dissolve in the water. Dissolved carbon dioxide makes water more acidic, and these deep parts of the ocean are just acidic enough to dissolve calcium-carbonate shells.

30. (A) Photosynthesis takes carbon dioxide from the air to make sugars and carbohydrates, while respiration does the reverse. Due to the enormous amount of carbon that plants, animals, and other organisms use every year, any imbalance of these two phenomena can cause pronounced differences in atmospheric carbon dioxide year to year.

31. (D) Only high-energy electrical discharges and nitrogen-fixing bacteria naturally create biologically usable nitrogen compounds.

32. (D) Destroying vegetation keeps an area from absorbing carbon dioxide through photosynthesis, while decaying plant matter releases more of the gas into the environment. At the same time, destruction of a vegetation-rich ecosystem releases nitrogen compounds all at once into the environment, while these molecules would ordinarily remain locked in organisms or be rapidly reabsorbed when released by small numbers of decaying organisms.

33. (C) Certain bacteria convert NH_3 to NO_2^- and NO_3^-. Plants can use NH_3 and NO_3^- but not NO_2^-.

34. (A) Nitric oxide, NO, from burning fossil fuels is converted to NO_2 and HNO_3—nitric acid—in the atmosphere, which can contribute to ocean acidification.

35. (C) The term describes the cycling of several different elements through the earth's organisms, atmosphere, soil, and rock. Biologists are generally most concerned with carbon, sulfur, nitrogen, water, and phosphorus.

36. (D) Like all organisms, plants break down carbohydrates and sugars for energy during respiration. Their photosynthesis creates these molecules using sunlight, and along with all other constituent molecules, these carbon-containing molecules break down into CO_2 and other products when they decompose.

37. (B) Ocean sediments and sedimentary rocks hold more than 1,000 times as much carbon as any other source.

38. (B) Decomposer bacteria break complex molecules, such as proteins, into smaller molecules and ultimately into nitrate and nitrite ions.

39. (A) Carbon is incorporated into the shells of marine organisms in the form of calcium carbonate. The shells can become part of seafloor sediment that is carried down into a subduction zone by a descending oceanic plate. When the plate reaches a depth at which melting begins to occur, the resulting magma can rise through the overlying plate and erupt through volcanoes. Some of the carbon in this magma comes from marine sediments.

   (B) Sulfur dioxide becomes oxidized to sulfur trioxide, and the addition of water changes it into sulfuric acid, H_2SO_4. This can reach land through acid deposition—acid rain—where sulfuric acid can be neutralized to become a sulfate salt, such as Na_2SO_4. Plants take up these salts and use their sulfur as a component of proteins.

(C) Carbon dioxide from volcanoes can enter organisms in the same way that other carbon dioxide does—it's incorporated into carbohydrates by plants and other photosynthetic organisms. Plants—or consumers—metabolize these carbohydrates for food and either incorporate the constituent carbon into other biological molecules, such as DNA, or release it as the waste product carbon dioxide.

40. (A) Limestone and other types of rock contain more calcium than any other natural source, and these are moved to the surface through tectonic plate movement. Calcium does not generally form large amounts of any gas spewed by volcanoes, and phytoplankton obtain calcium from the water.

41. (B) *Evaporation* is the process by which liquid water changes into a vapor. This occurs as solar energy adds latent heat to water molecules, which allows them to overcome molecular interactions with other water molecules and to escape into the air as vapor.

42. (B) The amount of sunlight that each zone receives is generally a function of its depth, with the abyssal zone getting the least light, and the euphotic getting the most.

43. (D) The littoral zone includes submerged soil near the surface along the edges and shallow areas of lakes.

44. (B) Nitrogen is very chemically unreactive, so the average N_2 molecule remains unchanged for a long time compared to compounds made with other biologically important elements.

45. (D) The *Gulf Stream* is a current that carries warm Caribbean water north past Canada to Europe.

46. (A) Along with tropical rain forests, swamps and estuaries have the highest net primary productivity of all ecosystems by far.

47. (A) Both tertiary consumers and secondary consumers eat other consumers, while primary consumers are herbivores and eat only plants.

48. (B) Rock is the major source of phosphate on land.

49. (D) Low nutrient levels, particularly of phosphate, keep algae populations in check. When more than enough nutrients are available, algae grow quickly and use up dissolved oxygen, a process that can suffocate many marine organisms.

50. (C) Whether in clouds, precipitation, runoff, or lakes and oceans, water remains H_2O throughout the water cycle.

51. (D) After evaporating from the ocean, some of this water is transported in the form of clouds that release precipitation over land.

52. (C) The radiant energy from the sun is largely responsible for evaporation, a key component in the hydrologic cycle.

53. (B) *Percolation* describes the flow of water to underground storage.

54. (C) *Transpiration* is evaporation from plants that have absorbed water, usually through their roots.

55. (A) In order for cloud droplets to form, water vapor needs a particle to collect on, such as dust.

Chapter 2: Living World: Biodiversity

56. (C) A greater diversity of genes confers a greater diversity of form and behavior.

57. (D) Each of these is a measure of diversity among organisms.

58. (C) Biologists gauge fitness in terms of offspring.

59. (C) An endemic species is unique to a defined geographic region. For example, American buffalo were once endemic to the North American West, while dodo birds were once endemic to Mauritius.

60. (C) Hot spots are a key part of the emergency plan to save as much terrestrial diversity as possible. Together they account for about two-thirds of such diversity.

61. (D) A habitat includes only the tangible elements of an organism's environment.

62. (C) Whitewater rafting would be considered a cultural ecosystem service. People enjoy rafting as an outdoor activity, and it increases both ecotourism and recreation.

63. (C) Genetic drift is essentially random, producing genetic diversity in greater or lesser amounts, whereas the other listed phenomena result only in less diversity.

64. (B) Two populations that trade members, and thus are genetically connected, are called a single *metapopulation*.

65. (C) Creatures with narrow niches are less able to switch to a new food source or a new type of shelter, for example.

66. (C) Longshore currents move sand along the beach and barrier islands.

67. (B) The smallest islands would have the fewest different habitats. This would cause the resources available to support diversity to decline as compared to a larger island. The smallest island would have less species richness than a larger island.

68. (A) The closest island will have a higher immigration rate since it is closer to the mainland and will have more species arriving than on an island farther away.

69. (B) The most biodiversity would exist on the largest island that is closest to the mainland and the original populations. Being closest to the mainland would allow more variety of plants and animals to immigrate to it. A larger island can support more habitats and more diverse species.

70. (D) The fundamental niche of an organism is the habitat range that it is able to inhabit, while the realized niche is what that organism can actually inhabit depending on environmental pressures.

71. (B) In this scenario, the only abiotic factor that changed in the tank was the addition of more aquatic plants. They provide more dissolved oxygen to the water, which helps the fish thrive and reproduce.

72. (A) Answer A would be correct since the lack of dissolved oxygen in the tank would be on the lower limit of tolerance range for the fish in the tank. The fish wouldn't have the abiotic factors (oxygen) that they needed to survive.

73. (D) The answer is D because too much sunlight would cause the population of smaller plants to decrease. The sunlight is at the upper limit of their tolerance range.

74. (C) The greatest amount of biodiversity would be found in the section with the highest range of tolerance.

75. (D) The pioneer species are able to survive in harsh environments and help to transform the environment to allow less tolerant species to live. Lichen is a common pioneer species. They will grow on bedrock and, over time, break it down into smaller pieces, eventually creating soil and room for plants to grow.

76. (B) Climax community is the final stage of succession. The organisms that are able to exist in this community will depend on the available resources.

77. (C) Logging is a human-caused (anthropogenic) ecological disturbance. All others occur without any input from humans.

78. (D) All of the biomes listed, except for tropical rainforest, need regular fires to help with seed germination, dispersal, and ecosystem renewal.

79. (B) Hurricanes do not cause tsunamis. They are caused by a sudden movement of the ocean surface by either an underwater earthquake, volcanic eruption, or underwater landslide.

80. (B) A bottleneck event has likely damaged genetic diversity, reducing the population mostly to green lizards.

81. (A) Beneficial mutations are rare, harmful mutations are more common, and harmless mutations are more common still.

82. (D) Evolution is generally identified through a change in allele frequencies in a population over time.

83. (D) Speciation is the formation of a new species from a splinter group, generally including a loss in the ability to reproduce with the larger original group.

84. (A) In evolutionary divergence, one species splits into several species that limit competition with each other.

85. (B) Secondary succession takes place when an ecosystem has been removed. Slash-and-burn agriculture creates this environment, and the diagram shows the growth that takes place following this event.

86. (C) Secondary succession is when the environment has been disturbed, but since the soil is still established, the ecosystem can rebound rather quickly from the disturbance.

87. (A) Lichens are a symbiotic relationship between a type of algae and fungi.

88. (C) Removing keystone species can disrupt big portions of the rest of an ecosystem.

89. (D) Trees are latecomers in colonizing an area, arriving only later in secondary succession. There is no tertiary succession.

90. (A) Lichens can live on bare rock with very little water and slowly extract nutrients from the rock, air, and passing debris.

Chapter 3: Populations

91. (C) Pandas are considered to be specialists. They live in a very specific habitat and have very specific dietary needs. They cannot survive outside of that narrow niche. Raccoons can eat a wider variety of foods and can adapt well to different environments.

92. (A) Commensalism is a relationship in which one partner benefits to neither the loss nor gain of the other partner.

93. (C) The honey badger is able to obtain food from a variety of sources, such as eating carrion and digging to find yams. If one food source were to be hard to find, the honey badger could adapt to a new source easily.

94. (D) K-selected species tend to colonize areas in late succession, have large offspring, and occupy a specialist niche in the ecosystem.

95. (B) A population is a large group of one species, while an ecosystem includes all interacting species.

96. (A) An r-selected species relies more on producing a quantity of smaller offspring that require less energy per individual to produce rather than single, large, long-lived offspring that require a relatively greater amount of energy per individual.

97. (C) Several variations exist, but the three general survivorship curves are constant loss, early loss, and late loss curves. These reflect the ages at which individuals of a species tend to die.

98. (A) Graph A is a population graph that represents an S-curve (logistic growth curve), which is indicative of a K-selected population. The population will grow at a slow and steady rate until it reaches the carrying capacity of the population in that environment, at which time the population should remain relatively stable.

99. (B) Songbirds exhibit Type II survivorship during their lifetime because they have a moderate death rate and the survival rate is constant.

100. (A) Humans exhibit Type I survivorship because humans have a low death rate and a higher survival rate in early and middle life.

101. (D) Turtles have a very high death rate early in life, but if they survive childhood, they will typically live long lives.

102. (D) Flooding is considered to be a natural disaster, which would limit a population size regardless of population density. It is a density-independent factor, while the other factors (competition, predation, and disease) will be affected by the population density.

103. (A) The ecological footprint is defined as the amount of land required to sustain an individual's use of natural resources.

104. (B) Overshoot is when the carrying capacity of a population is exceeded, which causes some of the population to compete for resources such as shelter, food, and mating partners. This competition will lead to a decrease in the population to a more sustainable size.

105. (C) Example C is a classic example of exponential growth. The growth of the population is not affected by any limiting factors. Those limiting factors could be things like population density or food availability.

106. (A) All of the answers are issues caused by population increase, but only A will be felt globally, as increased CO_2 emissions will contribute to climate change.

107. (C) "r" stands for the percentage rate of growth. For example, if the population is growing at a 5% rate, you would put 5 into the equation for "r".

108. (C) At and around point V, the curve's slope continues to increase as time passes.

109. (B) Population 1 enters logistic growth centered around the level of 10,000 individuals, which must be the carrying capacity.

110. (D) Population 1 varies from slightly above to slightly below 10,000 individuals without making major changes in either direction.

111. (A) Due to the later crash of Population 2, we can infer that its peak near point Z is above the environment's carrying capacity.

112. (D) Logistic growth tends to continue to approximate the environment's carrying capacity.

113. (D) Earthquakes affect individuals whether or not they are densely distributed. The other events occur more often in dense populations.

114. (B) Populations can fluctuate slightly and still be considered stable.

115. (B) Fecundity is an organism's reproductive capability, while fertility is the actual number of offspring it has produced.

116. (D) Clumping is the most common form of population distribution.

117. (C) Only births and immigrations add new individuals—*emigration* refers to individuals leaving a population.

118. (A) By definition, the environment cannot carry more individuals of a given species than its carrying capacity, so the population must come down.

119. (D) Logistic growth tends to keep populations varying slightly above and below the carrying capacity.

120. (C) $(100 + 20 - 10 + 30)$ mockingbirds/5 square kilometers = 28 mockingbirds per square kilometer.

121. (D) *Fecundity* refers to a species' reproductive potential—its ability. *Fertility* refers to the actual number of offspring an individual or population has produced. For example, although humans currently have the potential to have many children (fecundity), the fertility rate is fairly low due to birth control.

122. (D) The population density is a way to study the demographic features of a population in terms of how many people live in a given geographic area. Dhaka, Bangladesh, is the most densely populated city in the world, at 44,000 people per square kilometer.

123. (B) This population has a wider base (more children) than the top of the pyramid. In population pyramids that have a wide base, the population is growing rapidly because they are having more children.

124. (A) Age structure pyramids plot both age (range) and gender regarding the demographics of a particular country.

125. (C) Nigeria has a rapidly growing population, with more children being born than adults at the upper ages.

126. (D) Total impact is calculated by multiplying the other factors by one another, so $I = P \times A \times T$. I would increase fourfold if both P and A were doubled while keeping T the same.

127. (C) The replacement level fertility rate is the idea that the average woman needs to have 2.1 children in her lifetime in order to keep the population rate stable.

128. (A) As of 2019, Niger has the highest fertility rate in the world at 6.49 children per woman.

129. (D) *Life expectancy* is a statistical measure often used to determine future demographics by estimating how long individuals in a population will live.

130. (C) The most likely reason that Country X has larger age brackets at the younger end of its population is that the country has a higher birthrate than Country Y.

131. (A) With a disproportionately large segment of its population approaching retirement age, Country Y is likely to lose much of its tax base as older workers stop working and young workers do not replace them in comparable numbers.

132. (B) With a large segment of its population just below reproductive age and industrialization lowering its overall death rate, Country X is likely to grow more quickly in 15 years.

133. (C) With minor variations between age brackets, a constant loss survivorship curve would result in a population of decreasing numbers in older age brackets.

134. (B) With few exceptions, societies with slowing or stagnating growth rates are postindustrial.

135. (C) Lower birthrate results in fewer people in low-end age brackets. Emigration would result in mostly older people leaving the population, while immigration—with few associated births—would have to occur at a very high rate to result in such a lopsided age structure.

136. (A) The Great Plague was a density-dependent factor affecting certain people in England—those who lived closely together, especially in London. Diseases are less able to spread among widely spaced populations.
  (B) The Little Ice Age is a density-independent factor, since it affects a broad area of humans without regard to how close they live to one another.
  (C) The plague is the only biotic factor, while the Little Ice Age and the Great Fire of London are both abiotic factors.

137. (D) At the industrial level of development, human societies often have low birthrates, due to education of women and other factors, and low death rates, due to more advanced health care, safety standards, and other factors.

138. (D) Most developed nations besides the United States are projected to produce fewer babies than they already have older individuals, who have a higher death rate. That is, the large older population is expected to contribute to a higher death rate for these countries, and negative growth is likely to result from birthrates that can't match death rates. This can lead to resource allocation problems, such as a decreased tax base from which to draw social security funds.

139. (A) 2.0 children per couple is an ideal replacement number when no child dies, and all reach reproductive age. But 2.1 will take into account children dying before they are able to reproduce.

140. (D) Thomas Malthus hypothesized the idea that population growth is potentially exponential, while the growth of the food supply or other important resources would grow linearly. So, human population growth would exceed the available resources and the population would collapse.

141. (A) Education is the key to prevention for teenage pregnancies. If young people are educated and have access to contraceptives, you would have fewer pregnancies and fewer infant deaths overall.

142. (D) The correct order is pre-industrial, transitional, industrial, and post-industrial.

143. (A) In Stage 1 of the demographic transition, the birth rate and death rate are very high. A present example of this stage is Ethiopia.

144. (D) Stage 4 is considered the ideal stage, since the population rate is growing gradually, and the birth rate and death rate are relatively low.

145. (D) Due to a lack of population growth, the United States is currently in Stage 4 of the demographic transition.

146. (C) Degree of urbanization is calculated by dividing the city-dwelling population by the total population and then multiplying by 100% to obtain a percentage figure: $(20,000/1,000,000) \times 100\% = 2\%$.

147. (B) Since the total population remains constant, first calculate the change in the urban population: $(100 - 52) - (100 - 55) = (48 \text{ urban}) - (45 \text{ urban}) = 3$-person increase. Next, calculate the urban growth rate by dividing the change by the city's initial population—i.e., the population that it grew *from*—then multiply by 100% to obtain a percentage figure: $(3/45) \times 100\% = 6.7\%$.

148. (D) Urban sprawl causes an increase in water runoff from increased impervious cover, such as parking lots and streets.

149. (A) Developing countries have the highest current rate of urban growth.

150. (D) All of the other choices are "push" factors affecting immigration.

Chapter 4: Earth Systems and Resources

151. (D) Divergent faults pull away from each other, as magma slowly wells up from the mantle to fill the gap, forming new crust.

152. (A) Tectonic plates push against each other until enough pressure causes them to slip and grind violently against one another in the form of an earthquake.

153. (D) Sedimentary rock is formed from tiny pieces of debris—including debris from other rock types—settling together and eventually adhering together to form a solid mass.

154. (C) As a logarithmic scale, the Richter scale's earthquake-magnitude increments each indicate a tenfold increase from the previous increment.

155. (D) Subduction occurs when one plate is pushed into the earth's interior by another plate, forming a giant trench that runs along the fault.

156. (B) Undersea earthquakes cause ocean floor upheaval that results in tremendous waves.

157. (D) Earthquakes with magnitudes exceeding 7.0 on the Richter scale typically have Mercalli intensities of VIII and above. An intensity of XI is considered extreme with most masonry structures and bridges destroyed.

158. (D) Between 90% and 95% of volcanic gases are water vapor and carbon dioxide.

159. (D) Laterite soils, characterized by signification leaching and an accumulation of calcite and organic materials, develop in hot, tropical climates.

160. (D) Large marine mammals do not generally live in coastal wetlands but in the open ocean or in coastal areas that do not have enough vegetation to be considered a wetland.

161. (D) Some volcanoes form at hot spots in tectonic plates, but the majority form around the edges, such as in the Pacific Ocean's Ring of Fire.

162. (A) Phytoplankton float in the sun-drenched euphotic layer, where they can photosynthesize most efficiently.

163. (A) Because Yellowstone is not near a plate boundary, it's possible to deduce that the area lies over a hot spot.

(B) If previous eruptions occurred to the west and southwest of Yellowstone, then the North American plate is moving to the east and northeast over the hot spot.

(C) The large oval or circular areas are calderas. They form when a magma chamber expels its contents and the ground above it collapses to fill the resulting cavity.

164. (A) Earth's atmosphere is a mixture that is approximately 78% nitrogen, 21% oxygen, and 1% other gases.

165. (C) The Coriolis effect explains differences in the relative direction and speed of wind at different latitudes. Objects such as air molecules at the equator move rapidly relative to objects at higher and lower latitudes, since objects at the equator must move a greater total distance in a single rotation of the earth.

166. (A) The ozone layer within the stratosphere absorbs ultraviolet radiation from the sun. This increases the temperature in the upper stratosphere to temperatures greater than those in the lower stratosphere.

167. (B) As earth rotates on its axis, objects move at different linear speeds depending upon their latitudes. This is the Coriolis effect.

168. (D) An isobar on a weather map connects areas of equal atmospheric pressure (*iso-* = "equal," and *-bar* = "pressure").

169. (B) Physical weathering is the process by which a rock (or something else) is broken into smaller pieces without changing the chemical composition.

170. (D) Chemical weathering breaks substances down by changing their chemical composition. The process of hydrolysis chemically weathers through a reaction with water.

171. (D) Plants can break down rock by physical weathering, as roots push through rock, breaking it apart. Animals, such as worms or moles, may push through rock and soil, physically weathering as they go. Many plants and animals may secrete chemicals that will slowly weather a rock.

172. (D) The bedrock is the parent material of a soil profile. Often, large recognizable chunks of bedrock can be found partially weathered in the C horizon.

173. (D) The uppermost two layers of a soil profile make up the topsoil. These are the O horizon and the A horizon.

174. (A) The B horizon is beneath the A horizon. The A horizon is also referred to as the *zone of leaching* because materials such as soluble minerals are moved through the layer with water that passes through. The leached material ends up in the B horizon, making it the zone of accumulation.

175. (B) Pedocal soils are found in dry areas such as the western United States. These soils are characterized by significant accumulations of calcium carbonate.

176. (A) It is said that warm air can "hold more water" than cold air can. This is because the water molecules in warm air have more average kinetic energy and tend to remain in the gas state. When air cools, like it typically does at night, the air mass will cool and the water molecules will tend to condense into the liquid state.

177. (C) Frost wedging occurs when water falls into a crack in the rock and then freezes as temperatures drop. When the temperatures rise, more water enters into the now-larger crack, and when it refreezes, the crack is expanded farther. This is a type of mechanical weathering.

178. (B) The stratosphere contains the UV-protecting ozone layer.

179. (D) The ionosphere is the layer of atmosphere that exists from 30 to 600 miles above the earth's surface. It protects organisms on earth by absorbing some harmful extreme ultraviolet rays.

180. (C) The earth's atmosphere is made up of approximately 78% nitrogen gas.

181. (D) The rotation of the earth on its axis causes what is called the Coriolis effect. As an object moves above a spinning object, the trajectory will not follow a straight line.

182. (B) The leeward side of a mountain range is often dry and is where you can find the world's deserts. The windward side will get the most wind and rain.

183. (D) Hadley cells are a global climate phenomenon where warm weather near the tropics causes moisture to rise near the equator, cools as it rises, and descends in the subtropics. This process causes a global atmospheric circulation pattern.

184. (B) Convection is the phenomenon that causes warmer, usually moist air masses to rise and colder, more dense air masses to sink.

185. (D) The trade winds drive the dust clouds across the Atlantic Ocean and the Caribbean Sea.

186. (C) The jet stream

187. (D) *Channelization* is a method used to alter streams for uses such as flood control and improved drainage.

188. (B) *Dendritic drainage* is a term used to describe the branching pattern of streams. Many small streams contribute to the tributaries that eventually drain into large rivers.

189. (A) Sand is the largest of the three soil particles. Sand particles maintain more air space, which would allow water to drain most easily. Clay is the smallest particle, with loam being in between sand and clay in size.

190. (B) The largest freshwater aquifer in the world is the Ogallala Aquifer. It underlies an estimated 174,000 square miles of the Central Plains of the United States and is currently being depleted at a rapid rate by groundwater removal.

191. (A) Water in the Atlantic Ocean is not warm enough to support hurricane formation until June, and it can stay above the threshold temperature of 25°C until November.
  (B) Global warming could result in greater hurricane incidence. According to some models, Atlantic water temperature would rise with average global temperatures, extending hurricane season or increasing the number of hurricanes per year.
  (C) When examined over a long period of time, overall hurricane incidence has not changed significantly with changes in climatic conditions.

192. (A) Earth's seasons are caused by changes in the angle of incoming solar radiation as the earth orbits the sun while tilting on its axis.
  (B) During summer in the Northern Hemisphere, the earth is farthest from the sun, but the planet's axis tilts toward it. Sunlight strikes the Northern Hemisphere in the summer at an angle that is closer to perpendicular, resulting in high solar intensity. Although the earth is closest to the sun during the winter, its axis tilts away from the star, so the sun's rays strike the Northern Hemisphere at a shallow angle that results in less light per unit area.
  (C) The climate of a particular spot on earth is dependent upon the weather and the precipitation. These factors vary widely based on the season.

193. (C) The tilt of the earth on its axis is the reason for different seasons on earth. Different latitudes receive various amounts of direct or indirect sunlight.

194. (B) Some insolation (solar radiation) gets absorbed by gases up in the atmosphere, while some will reach earth's surface without interference. Collisions with gas molecules and dust in the atmosphere will help to scatter it as well.

195. (A) Trade winds are deflected toward and found near the equator.

196. (C) Climate is defined as a region's weather patterns over a long period of time.

197. (B) The amount of precipitation and temperature are the two variables that determine the region's climate.

198. (C) This biome is characterized by low precipitation and high temperatures year-round.

199. (D) A tropical rainforest is characterized by high temperatures and high precipitation year-round.

200. (B) Biomes are determined primarily by temperature and the amount of rainfall, known as precipitation. As elevation increases, temperature decreases and rainfall (precipitation) tends to increase.

201. (A) Sunspots are caused by intense magnetic activity in the sun. These bursts of energy most impact the outermost layer of earth's atmosphere, the thermosphere.

202. (C) The changing seasons on earth are caused by the 23.5° tilt of earth's axis and the movement of earth in its orbit around the sun. The distance between earth and the sun does not cause the earth's seasons.

203. (C) An Atlantic hurricane begins off the coast of Africa with a drop in barometric pressure. This may then build into a tropical depression, which can eventually become a hurricane under the right conditions.

204. (D) When people refer to the *relative humidity* on a certain day, they are discussing the connection between the temperature of the air and the amount of water vapor in the air.

205. (D) A *temperature inversion* is a condition in the lower atmosphere where a stable layer of warm air lies above a layer of cooler air. This frequently occurs in valleys and basins.

206. (D) The troposphere is the layer of the atmosphere closest to earth's surface. It is this layer that life on earth depends upon. This is where most of our weather occurs.

207. (B) An ENSO event (El Niño-Southern Oscillation) is one in which the temperature of the eastern Pacific Ocean surface experiences a change of more than 0.5°C for longer than five months. These events occur regularly, about every two to seven years, lasting for a period of one to two years.

208. (C) A year in which El Niño is occurring will see warmer than normal water moving eastward to reach the western coast of South America.

209. (A) El Niño and La Niña events are near opposites. Both involve changes in Pacific Ocean surface temperatures, with La Niña involving cool temperatures and El Niño involving warm surface temperatures. Both phenomena change rainfall patterns in parts of the world differently.

210. (D) An ENSO impacts the weather around the globe. ENSO years may see droughts in the western Pacific, floods in lands around the eastern Pacific, and a decrease in Atlantic hurricanes.

Chapter 5: Land and Water Use

211. (D) Cluster development concentrates housing and leaves large areas of land open for recreation or other uses.

212. (A) The United States first established national parks to protect undeveloped natural areas and the species that live there. At Yellowstone, this includes the park's incredible geysers, canyons, prairies, forests, and wide diversity of animal and plant species.

(B) Hunters are generally not allowed to kill animals in U.S. national parks. This prohibition has helped the endangered bison and grizzly bears of the West to survive.

(C) The U.S. National Park Service administers and maintains the country's national parks.

(D) Tourism is one of the main threats—even well-meaning visitors erode trails and leave waste behind that degrades the natural environment. The more visitors, the more degradation generally takes place. Surrounding developed areas also threaten national parks through air and water pollution crossing into parkland, as well as the introduction of nonnative species.

213. (B) Overfishing and deforestation are examples of the overuse of open-access renewable resources.

214. (C) *Selective cutting* is deliberately thinning mature trees in order to leave a seed source for new tree growth and provide habitat as well.

215. (D) The United States has the largest old-growth forest in the world, located in Alaska.

216. (D) Clear-cutting is considered to be the most efficient and economical way to harvest trees to be used as lumber in a specific area. Because access is all at once, it is considered to be less harmful to the environment.

217. (A) Nitrogen-containing organic matter, such as dead plant and animal material and topsoil, is often washed out to sea. Even if bacteria can convert organic material in the ground and nitrogen gas in the air into nitrates that plants can use, much of this is lost in runoff.

(B) With little of the vegetation it once had, Madagascar doesn't contribute as much water vapor to the hydrologic cycle as it once did through transpiration and evaporation from land. Instead, a great deal of water runs off the land nearly unimpeded into rivers and out to sea.

(C) With less usable nitrogen and captured water in the soil, plants are not able to grow as quickly, so Madagascar's plants as a whole capture less carbon dioxide as they photosynthesize carbohydrates. At the same time, a great deal of carbon-containing organic material is lost in runoff, so the island doesn't contribute as much carbon dioxide to the carbon cycle from organic matter decaying on land. Instead, this ends up as carbon dioxide that joins the biological carbon cycle once it is broken down in the sea.

218. (B) Drought is a natural event. Land degradation occurs primarily with unsound human practices.

219. (A) Three signs of desertification are reduced water in ponds and streams, increased erosion, and lowering of the water table.

(B) Two specific examples of people's contribution to desertification include too much farming in an area and deforestation of an area for timber.

(C) Instead of overfarming, people could practice crop rotation and leave some areas fallow so their fertility can be restored. Also, instead of deforesting an area for timber, local people could utilize the forests for other products such as coffee, medicine, and native crops, leaving the forest intact. They could meet their needs by trading with each other or by partnering with Western countries to provide these goods for sale outside the country.

220. (B) *Silent Spring* was written by marine biologist Rachel Carson. It pointed out the environmental contamination caused by careless use of pesticides and herbicides.

221. (B) The soil of grasslands has a lot of organic content from decaying plant material.

222. (D) Crop rotation is the process of rotating crop families in the same plot of soil over several years to allow different crops to use and replenish different soil nutrients naturally. This decreases the need for artificial fertilizers and pesticides.

223. (D) Biological diversity is decreased due to loss of competing ecosystems, not increased.

224. (A) Overgrazing of animals is the single largest issue with land/soil management issues and desertification around the world.

225. (D) Feedlots are places where cattle are kept in large quantities in small spaces. Their waste often pollutes local water supplies.

226. (C) People in China are consuming more meat than before, which requires more grain to be produced to feed the livestock.

227. (A) High percentages of soybean crops, cotton crops, and corn crops are genetically modified.

228. (A) Bottom trawling is a method in which a net is dragged along the bottom of the ocean to catch fish, but it often catches many unintended species. Discarding bycatch is used when fish that are caught but are the wrong type or size are thrown back overboard; but often they are dead before they can be returned.

(B) The development of better fishing gear that doesn't trap so many unwanted species from the bottom is one method of preventing overfishing. Also, raising fish on farms may prevent breeding stocks from getting depleted.

229. (B) Topsoil, called the A horizon, has both organic and inorganic materials, holds moisture well, and supports crop growth. This A horizon is beneath the thin O horizon which is the thin, top layer consisting primarily of leaf litter and humus.

230. (D) By rotating different crops and allowing the land to "rest" or be left fallow from harvest occasionally, farmers reduce the prevalence of disease and prevent the soil from getting depleted of nutrients.

231. (B) Using reclaimed water, preventing runoff, and using dry cooling systems in industrial processes are all methods that help conserve water, also known as *conservation*.

232. (D) Land that drains to the same lake or river is known as a *watershed*, or *runoff zone*.

233. (D) Resources such as groundwater that are being consumed faster than they can be resupplied are said to be *nonrenewable*.

234. (B) The water table is the upper level of groundwater and is found at the upper edge of the zone of saturation and the bottom edge of the zone of aeration of the soil.

235. (D) Drip irrigation is the most efficient way to provide water directly to a plant's roots and reduce runoff and waste.

236. (C) A *water budget* is *precipitation − evaporation = runoff*. This is a model that includes input, output, and storage of water.

237. (D) Strip cropping is a farming method in which two different crops are alternated in strips on the same plot of land so that one crop can slow the runoff of water from the other and also act as a wind barrier.

238. (A) Conventional agriculture regularly uses synthetic herbicides, pesticides, and fertilizers. Sustainable agriculture avoids these substances and instead substitutes solutions that have a smaller impact on the environment. These solutions include removing weeds by hand or using natural herbicides, controlling insect pests with insect predators, and using compost in place of chemical fertilizers.
  (B) Conventional agriculture can spoil the land by destroying habitats as the area is cleared for agriculture; using fertilizer, pesticides, and herbicides, which can contaminate the groundwater; and exposing the soil to further erosion.
  (C) Sustainable agriculture avoids disruption of the land by maintaining natural ecosystems; by not clearing entire areas, and thus not leaving the land bare; by planting diverse crops, using natural fertilizers, and preventing chemical pollution of land and water; and by consuming less energy for chemical fertilizers and other synthetic substances.

239. (C) Subsistence crops are grown by the farmer primarily to directly meet the farmer's own food needs.

240. (D) Perennial crops, which grow from the same root system each year, have many ecological benefits despite having slightly lower productivity.

241. (C) A limiting factor is the one nutrient a crop needs that is in the shortest supply.

242. (C) Approximately 60% of the pesticides found in our waters come from herbicides, the largest share of any of the pesticides.

243. (A) Traditional herding involves letting cows roam freely over grazing land. If their numbers are not too great, this benefits the area because manure acts as a fertilizer, and the grazing stimulates plant growth. This practice is a problem only if the number of cows is too high and the plants are overgrazed to the point that they don't regenerate. Industrial grazing is the same in the beginning. The cattle roam and graze freely, hurting only the environment if the numbers are too large. The major problems occur after that, when the cattle are sent to feedlots. Manure becomes a source of water pollution because of its volume. In addition, gases that are produced by the manure contribute to global warming, the soil may become damaged with salts and trace elements, and the spread of pathogens to humans becomes more viable.

(B) When nonnative grazing animals are introduced to an area of rangeland, the native vegetation may be overgrazed until it's gone because the ecosystem is not used to this species. In addition, if there are other grazing animals on the land, they may have to compete with the new species for food, and their numbers may decrease, or the native species may even be eliminated.

(C) To manage the farm sustainably, it is important to follow these principles of rangeland management:

1. Limit the number of cattle so that the land can regenerate.
2. Rotate the areas that are grazed so their fertility can be restored.
3. Distribute the cattle in different areas and fence off overused areas.
4. Restore the land that has been used by reseeding and fertilizing the vegetation.
5. Improve the land with controlled burns to restore fertility and rid the land of unwanted plants.

244. (D) Purse-seining is the fishing method that uses a large net and closes the top of the net (like a purse) to enclose the fish.

245. (C) When using large-scale fishing techniques, some fishermen catch things that were not intended, such as dolphins, turtles, and even seabirds. These are considered "bycatch" and are often just thrown back overboard.

246. (A) Strip mining is a process in which machines, explosives, or both are employed to remove horizontal layers of earth from a mineral-rich area. Used most often to recover coal and tar sands, strip mining an area uncovers rich seams of the desired material that already lie near the surface. Miners process the removed earth to extract desired materials and discard the remaining waste.

(B) Miners often discard waste earth in nearby rivers and streams that take the waste away. This waste material often contains previously buried poisonous heavy metals such as arsenic, petroleum products from mining machines, and wastewater and sewage from mining facility buildings. Particulate matter often accumulates in nearby streams and can completely bury them, destroying both the streams and the ecosystems that previously relied upon them. At the surface, strip mining completely destroys any ecosystem that previously existed at the site, such as a pine forest or the stream that currently exists at the site of the planned Chuitna project.

(C) The Surface Mining Control and Reclamation Act of 1977 would require PacRim to attempt some environmental restoration only at the end of the Chuitna Coal Project, which might occur after the project's first 25-year phase, at the very soonest.

247. (D) Placer mining involves using water to wash away unwanted materials.

248. (A) Gillard's goal of increasing job opportunities in outer suburbs will likely increase sprawl around those existing suburbs, unless Australian regional and local governments structure policies to specifically prevent further suburban development.

(B) Each person in a densely constructed urban area can more quickly and easily reach housing, shopping, medical facilities, transportation options, and other needs. In spread-out suburbs, reaching many of these amenities may require a long drive or walk.

(C) Since urban areas with more community services can more efficiently serve a greater number of people, the funding shortfalls in bad economic times have less of an effect on services per person than in spread-out areas.

249. (D) Heat and carbon dioxide do not increase local rainfall levels, but the other three factors do contribute to urban flooding.

250. (D) Sewage doesn't do much to increase calcium in oceans and lakes, and calcium doesn't pose a danger to fish and shellfish.

251. (C) Greenbelt provides space for recreation and plant and animal habitats in cities like Toronto.

252. (A) Mixed-use development involves integrating housing, work, and other components of a person's daily life within walking distance.

253. (A) The U.S. government provided the first three inducements, but it does not typically fund whole suburban developments, and certainly not on a large regional scale.

254. (C) Cities have all of the effects indicated except significantly decreasing cloud formation. In fact, particulate matter that cities release into the atmosphere can encourage nearby cloud formation.

255. (A) Improving pest control, disease resistance, transport, and storage would help offset the losses of almost one-third of agricultural crops.

256. (D) When too much groundwater is used up in coastal areas, salt groundwater moves into fresh groundwater, and surface water declines as well.

257. (A) Preparing a building site produces loose sediment that is washed away in heavy rainfall.

258. (D) An influent stream is above the water table and is refilled only by precipitation.

259. (C) Since water holds up the soil, when groundwater is removed, the soil sinks, and this process is known as *subsidence*.

260. (A) An example of a natural event that contributes to flooding includes a situation in which the land has little vegetation, causing the precipitation to run off the surface, as it does in flash floods in the desert. Man-made changes that contribute to flooding include deforestation from logging and also paving of surfaces in urban areas, both of which increase surface runoff.

(B) Two methods of flood control that are currently in use in the United States include levees and streambed channelization. Levees hold water back from flooding an area. This is a problem because if they fail, there is nothing else to prevent destruction. Streambed channelization occurs when the sides of a river are bulldozed to make them wider and allow more water to flow. This damages habitats, causes erosion, and creates flooding somewhere else.

(C) The Watershed Protection and Flood Prevention Act of 1954 approached the flooding issue with the idea of draining wetlands. This took care of the problem in the immediate area but then caused flooding in other places.

(D) To implement watershed management, there are several methods that can be employed. Development should be limited, and areas that have been deforested should be replanted. Also, surface runoff should be diverted to holding areas.

261. (C) Biological pest control employs natural resources, such as predators, to minimize the impact of pests on crops.

262. (B) One of the biggest disadvantages of using pesticides is that pests can develop resistance that either causes the pesticide to become ineffective or will cause the farmer to have to use more in order to be as effective.

263. (D) *Terracing* is the practice of taking one very large, very steep field and breaking it into many smaller fields. This helps prevent large amounts of soil from eroding from the surface.

264. (B) Contour plowing is the process of planting crops along equal elevations on a hill rather than up and down the hill. This slows down the runoff of water.

265. (D) Technological advancements have allowed for increased human population over the past few hundred years. The human population is the biggest factor in environmental degradation.

266. (D) Public service functions of forests are benefits that humanity receives from the forest just by the forest's existing. Harvesting timber requires work and is not simply a by-product of the forest's existence.

267. (A) Indirect deforestation occurs when trees die from causes other than logging. Pollution, disease, and global warming are possible causes of indirect deforestation.

268. (B) Sustainable forestry practices involve cutting only enough trees so that the ecosystem recovers and the following year it is possible to cut the same amount of trees.

269. (C) Forest fires are beneficial in opening cones to release seeds, removing brush, replenishing soil, and *preventing* crown fires from occurring, not causing them.

270. (C) Minimum tillage is a farming technique that reduces the manipulation of the soil. This significantly reduces soil erosion because the soil is held in place by crops or residues of crops.

Chapter 6: Energy Resources and Consumption

271. (B) Coal, oil, and natural gas are nonrenewable resources.

272. (C) Conventional and unconventional oil types do not differ significantly in carbon dioxide released upon burning. However, the processing steps necessary for converting some unconventional oil sources into usable forms can release huge amounts of carbon dioxide on their own.

273. (B) Solar energy is renewable and will last as long as the sun—assuming unobstructed skies. Natural gas supplies are projected to last between 60 and 125 years, while conventional oil supplies are projected to last 30 to 60 more years.

274. (A) Peat is a fossil fuel, since it consists of ancient, compressed plant matter that cannot be quickly replenished. Biomass is recently produced plant matter and is a renewable resource.
   (B) As a lower-quality, dirtier-burning coal, bituminous is composed of a lower proportion of carbon by weight than anthracite. But it has a much higher carbon content than peat, since it has been compressed and chemically converted into coal from ancient peat. (Bituminous coal's exact carbon content varies from 77% to 87%.)
   (C) Most likely not. The ancient Irish lake completely filled with plant matter long ago, and it no longer maintains a thin layer of water that would support plant growth and accumulation of dead plant matter, as well as the occasional addition of a sedimentary layer. Second, human interference has drained the bog and removed most of the peat.

275. (A) In 2003, Canada's bitumen—or tar sands—deposits were reclassified as oil deposits.

276. (D) Middle Eastern countries have about 66% of the world's total oil supply beneath them.

277. (B) Conversion in this case involves sunlight passing through the window, in which some energy is reflected and lost as heat. Inside the room, almost all of the sunlight becomes heat. All the other choices involve several steps in which energy is expended in conversion.

278. (A) Geothermal power is derived from the heat of the earth's interior.

279. (C) Natural gas "floats" above petroleum deposits in the earth, and it contains all these gases, with methane in the largest amount.

280. (D) Like all fossil fuels, burning natural gas results in release of carbon dioxide.

281. (A) Contour strip mining is used to remove coal from hilly and mountainous terrain.

282. (A) Natural gas is transported in special pressurized pipelines or in containers once it has been cooled to a low enough temperature to liquefy.

283. (A) Deuterium and tritium are two isotopes of hydrogen. Where normal hydrogen has only a proton in each atomic nucleus, a deuterium atom contains one proton and one neutron in each nucleus, and a tritium atom contains one proton and two neutrons.

(B) The plasma is very, very hot and would melt any physical object touching it. This would probably also cause some of the plasma to cool enough to become merely hot hydrogen gas.

(C) Like most types of nuclear reactors, this General Fusion prototype will use heat—in this case, from hot liquid metal—to turn water into steam, which will drive electricity-generating turbines.

284. (B) Hydroelectric power is second to fossil fuel use in global energy production.

285. (B) The United States is the largest user of nuclear power in the world.

286. (D) The flow will decrease, and the prices will increase globally.

287. (A) Some energy is lost as heat at each and every processing step involved in changing coal from one form to another.

(B) The price of petroleum-based fuels would have to rise above that of coal-derived liquid fuels, including the price of infrastructure needed to produce the new fuels. This can happen due to petroleum's becoming more expensive to produce or as a result of its becoming more difficult to obtain—for example, due to an embargo by oil-producing nations. Also, the price of competing fuels, such as biomass-based ethanol, would probably also have to be very high in order for liquid-coal fuels to become a competitive option.

(C) Unburned fuels such as gasoline are highly toxic, and many contain carcinogens. Incomplete combustion can also produce dangerous gases such as carbon monoxide as well as environmentally damaging products, including nitrous oxide.

(D) Coal-derived fuel would still release about as much carbon dioxide as petroleum-based fuel when it is burned, in addition to the considerable land-use, pollution, and health hazards involved in coal mining.

288. (A) Under controlled conditions, bacteria can convert biomass, such as wood, leaves, and other plant parts, to methane, methanol, or ethanol.

289. (D) The more steps between an energy source's original form and its final use, the more energy is lost along the way. Here energy is lost burning the biomass, heating water to steam, turning the turbine for electricity, making hydrogen from water, and burning hydrogen in an automobile. Other choices use some of these same steps but fewer of them.

290. (B) Only organic materials are useful as biomass fuel.

291. (A) In 2019, the world's two most populous nations: China and India were also the two largest coal-consuming countries. The United States comes in third in the world for coal consumption.

292. (B) Burning natural gas for energy results in fewer emissions of air pollutants and greenhouse gases (such as CO_2).

293. (D) Drilling in ANWR would not be worth the risk. There is so much potential for environmental harm, while the benefits are low. Opponents feel as though we should focus on developing more sustainable energy solutions for our future.

294. (D) All answers are considered passive except for D. D uses photovoltaic cells to create electricity, which is then used to do work.

295. (A) In these systems, the net energy yield is low compared to other systems. Because heat is being collected, a lot of energy is lost to the surrounding environment.

296. (D) Although energy production is considered to be greenhouse gas-free, the production of the panels does cause some emissions from mining, production, and distribution.

297. (B) Depending on local conditions, underground heat can be depleted for a period of time that is significant to people, such as a period of months or years. To slow heat depletion, some facilities that use geothermal steam will pump used hot water back into underground reservoirs.

298. (A) Hoover Dam is an impoundment dam, since it retains water in a reservoir, letting a controlled, high-pressure stream out to do work. In the case of Hoover Dam, the water stream runs turbines that generate electricity.

(B) Yes. Lake Mead fills with water from upstream rainfall and melting snow, which are replenished by natural processes.

(C) Lake Mead consumed a large area of land that once featured plants and animals belonging to the local desert ecosystem. Also, the dam prevents the flow of nutrients to downriver areas, and it interferes with local aquatic ecosystems, such as those of river fish.

299. (A) Geothermal energy comes from the earth's interior, and the energy is independent of the sun.

300. (B) The disadvantages of geothermal energy are mainly that the power plants are expensive to build, the energy output may be inconsistent, and geothermal sites may just run out of steam after years of activity.

301. (D) Geothermal energy is generated in over 20 countries. The largest producer of geothermal energy worldwide is the United States.

302. (D) With the extremely low melting temperature of $-259.14°C$—about 14 K—hydrogen would require too much energy to freeze for storage.

303. (B) Uranium-238 is nonfissionable, and it makes up about 97% of the uranium in reactor fuel.

304. (B) The splitting of an atomic nucleus is called *fission*.

305. (C) Radioactive decay in the core causes nearby materials to become radioactive themselves, and in the process, it changes the constituent elements of these materials, making them weaker and more likely to crack, break, and fall apart.

306. (D) Radioactive particles release ionizing radiation, which consists of very fast-moving particles that directly damage a cell's DNA. Radiation can also ionize water, which releases free radicals that also damage DNA. Damaged DNA affects the way a cell operates and reproduces.

307. (D) A breeder reactor produces fissionable fuel by adding neutrons to nonfissionable material. A breeder reactor can convert uranium-238 into plutonium-239, for example.

308. (A) Dams are useful to people, despite the environmental destruction that ensues. First, dams store water for future use. This is especially important to ensure an adequate water supply for people in regions with little precipitation and also as the population continues to grow. Second, dams provide hydroelectric power to cities, offsetting the need for fossil fuels and therefore reducing carbon emissions. Third, dams provide recreation areas for people for activities such as fishing, boating, and waterskiing. These areas bring in tourist revenue for local towns and also provide jobs.

(**B**) Dear residents of Springfield,

As you know, voters will be deciding the fate of the new dam in the upcoming election. I am writing to you today to urge you to vote "no" on this measure for several reasons. We can learn from the example of the Three Gorges Dam in China what impact the proposed dam could have on the future of Springfield. First, flooding is a major issue. People in China built settlements downstream from the dam despite the fact that they were in a potential flood-prone area. This is especially problematic since the area is susceptible to earthquakes and has already experienced major landslides. In addition, the sedimentation of the river is destroying the habitat of endangered species and contributing to the previously mentioned risk of flooding. The river that supplies the dam is already being polluted with sewage, which stagnates in the dam. Hundreds of thousands of residents were relocated to build Three Gorges Dam and were never compensated. Archaeological sites became flooded, and the beauty of the land was forever altered. Is this the future we want for the town of Springfield? Please vote "no" on construction of the Springfield dam.

(**C**) Although there are some advantages to having a dam, there are many ways to manage the water supply to avoid the need for new dams. First, the number of people in arid regions must be limited if possible. This includes not developing land for housing in areas that don't have an adequate water supply. Second is water conservation. Irrigation systems in agricultural areas need to be updated to use the most efficient and conservative methods. Crops that require a lot of water should not be grown in dry regions. Industrial water use should be updated to be efficient as well. Individuals should change their habits in their own homes, including watering landscape at the right time of day and in moderation and installing low-water-use showerheads, toilets, and washing machines. Third, cities should recycle water and irrigate the public landscape with recycled wastewater. And last, governments can assist by offering incentives for water conservation and passing laws that mandate watering restrictions and higher rates for excessive water use.

309. (D) Spent nuclear fuel rods are not radioactive enough to create a nuclear explosion, but they are radioactive enough to heat up well beyond the flash point of their constituent materials. If this happens, the resulting fire will release radioactive gases and dust into the environment.

310. (A) Only the "closed" nuclear fuel cycle involves reprocessing spent fuel into usable fuel.

311. (B) Direct emissions from a hydrogen fuel cell are just water and a little heat.

312. (C) Earth has no transuranium elements of its own. Natural occurrences of these elements, such as plutonium-239, have all undergone radioactive decay since earth's formation—if they were even present then. People produce these elements by means of nuclear physics, including bombarding heavy-element atoms with neutrons in breeder reactors.

313. (D) Reprocessing of nuclear waste releases some carbon dioxide, but not much compared with energy generated by burning fossil fuels. Normal nuclear power plant operations release very little air pollution.

314. (B) Elements of the nuclear fuel cycle each deal directly with radioactive materials. Decommissioning of power plants, mining ore, and temporary storage of radioactive waste are three components of the *open* nuclear fuel cycle. Reprocessing nuclear waste is an element of the *closed* cycle.

315. (D) Coal plants are very dirty, but they are relatively simple compared to nuclear power plants, and even with pollution-reducing technology, they require fewer safety measures and less maintenance.

316. (D) Scientists are constantly working on improving fusion reactor designs, but so far no one has made a reactor that produces more power from fuel than is expended during the process.

317. (A) The rods had probably already cracked enough to contaminate the water, and they would probably have continued to contaminate the water further, creating more waste for the plant to dispose of. With even less water circulation, the rods might have caused enough steam to build up to trigger a steam explosion, which could damage the containment pool. If the rods became uncovered, they could heat up enough to catch on fire, releasing radioactive gases into the air.

(B) Allowing fission fuel pellets to gather too close to one another could cause an uncontrolled fission reaction, which could very quickly cause a steam explosion and a fire, releasing radioactive gases into the air.

(C) Boron can absorb neutrons that hit its atomic nuclei. This would decrease the number of neutrons emitted by uranium fuel pellets that collide with the atomic nuclei of uranium elsewhere nearby. This would slow the overall rate of nuclear fission and cool the fuel and its surroundings.

318. (A) Photovoltaic cells produce electrical current when exposed to light.

319. (D) *Hydroelectric power* is the general term for electricity generated by damming the flow of a river and using the water to turn turbines.

320. (C) Dams often have a negative impact on the environment, including flooding land, which destroys habitat, and decreasing the flow of fertilizer—in the form of silt—below a dam.

321. (A) About two-thirds of the energy released by burning ethanol must be consumed in running the agricultural and processing machinery required for making the fuel.

322. (D) Some U.S. homeowners have opted to pipe water underground, where temperatures usually hover at around 10°C (or about 50°F), and back. In the winter in cold regions, this water requires less heat to become hot than water straight from the tap. In the summer, the water can be run through the small pipes of a heat exchanger, which blows indoor air across them to remove heat.

323. (B) Wind turbine power output is proportional to the area swept by its blades. Doubling the swept area doubles the energy a turbine can capture.

324. (D) Along with other electricity-generating devices that rely on rotational motion, wind turbines generate alternating current.

325. (D) When the wind blows past a wind turbine, its blades capture the wind's energy and rotate, turning it into mechanical energy. The mechanical energy turns a generator, which creates electrical energy.

326. (A) China is the world leader in wind energy.

327. (A) The nuclear power plants emit very little, if any, carbon dioxide into the atmosphere. However, the processes in the nuclear fuel chain, such as the mining and enrichment of ore and waste management, will add greenhouse gases to the atmosphere.

328. (C) The CAFE standards are set for domestic passenger vehicles, not commercially used vehicles, such as semi-trailer trucks.

329. (A) In 2017, the (CAFE) standards were more than 38 miles per gallon for domestic and imported passenger vehicles.

330. (D) 100 watts × 4 hours = 400 watts. A kilo is equal to 1,000.

Chapter 7: Atmospheric Pollution

331. (D) Smog levels are highest in summer because the reactions that form smog are affected by sunlight, and the air is relatively hot and slow moving in summer.

332. (D) Chlorofluorocarbons (CFC) are anthropogenic sources, which means they are "man-made." The rest occur naturally.

333. (D) Humans live in the troposphere. Pollution in the troposphere can affect our lungs, eyes, heart, and skin. It can be harmful and even deadly to humans, animals, and plants.

334. (A) The Union Carbide pesticide plant in Bhopal, India, released highly toxic gases. These gases were dense, so they stayed low to the ground. This caused many deaths and other respiratory health issues in the surrounding area.

335. (B) Nitrogen dioxide is defined as one of the six criteria pollutants in outdoor air by the Clean Air Act.

336. (C) National Ambient Air Quality Standards (NAAQS) specify the maximum amounts of sulfur dioxide to be present in outdoor air. Sulfur dioxide can cause major respiratory issues.

337. (D) Particles in the PM 2.5 size range are small enough to be able to travel deeply into the respiratory tract, ultimately getting into the lungs. Exposure to these fine particles can cause short- and long-term health effects such as trouble breathing, asthma, lung, and heart disease.

338. (D) The atmospheric pollutants or gases that form smog are released in the air when fossil fuels are burned. Smog is formed when heat (sunlight), gases, and particulates are combined.

339. (B) Photochemical smog happens when vehicle exhaust and volatile organic compounds (VOCs) react together in the presence of sunlight (heat).

340. (B) "London smog" results from a high concentration sulfur-bearing fossil fuels (like coal).

341. (D) As of 2020, India had the world's worst air pollution.

342. (D) Los Angeles is home to the U.S. city with the worst smog because of the number of vehicles (exhaust) and many days with sunshine.

343. (B) A thermal inversion happens when a layer of cooler air is held closest to the earth's surface, and a warmer layer of air holds it down and traps pollutants nearest to the ground. This increases air pollution issues.

344. (A) The AQI (air quality index) ranges from 0 to 500. Human health issues increase with the number. An AQI value over 300 represents very dangerous air quality and can cause human (and animal) health problems.

345. (D) The Great Smog blanketed the British capital of London for five days in December 1952. Over 12,000 people were killed in this pollution event.

346. (D) Los Angeles/Long Beach ranks first for high ozone days out of 225 metropolitan U.S. cities.

347. (D) Photochemical smog can contribute to health issues such as respiratory and heart disease.

348. (A) The oceans act as a major reservoir of carbon dioxide.

349. (D) When plants photosynthesize, they increase their usage and storage of carbon dioxide, thus decreasing it from the atmosphere.

350. (D) Decreasing our fossil fuel consumption would dramatically decrease the atmospheric carbon dioxide emissions.

351. (C) Carbon stored in carbonate shells in the ocean has the longest residence time.

352. (D) Particulate matter (PM) consists of fine to small particulates that are suspended in the atmosphere. The biggest contributors are power plants and other industrial processes, including the burning of fossil fuels.

353. (B) The oldest continuous ice core record is over 800,000 years in Antarctica.

354. (B) Carbon monoxide is produced by the burning of fossil fuels in an enclosed space without sufficient oxygen and ventilation.

355. (B) Exposure to radon is the second leading cause of lung cancer in the United States.

356. (A) Legionella bacteria are waterborne bacteria that can thrive in air-conditioning units, and they can multiply rapidly causing a fatal type of pneumonia if the conditions are right.

357. (B) If you were to inhale asbestos, the tiny fibers could enter your airway. Those tiny fibers can lodge deep within your lungs. This can cause cancer to develop.

358. (B) Radon is a colorless, odorless gas that forms from alpha decay of uranium.

359. (B) The Kyoto Protocol, signed in Kyoto, Japan, became international law in 2005. The goal of the law is to reduce carbon dioxide (CO_2) and other dangerous greenhouse gas emissions (GHG) in the atmosphere.

360. (C) The Clean Air Act of 1963 is a U.S. federal law designed to control air pollution on a national level.

361. (C) Nuclear energy is one of the cleanest sources of energy in the United States. Nuclear power emits no greenhouse gases when generating electricity.

362. (B) An electrostatic precipitator uses electricity to remove particles from a gas stream. When the plates are electrified, the charged particles in the gas are attracted to the collector plates.

363. (D) Wet scrubbers send pollution (exhaust gases) through a large cylinder that sprays a liquid (usually water) to clean the air.

364. (D) "Clean" or unpolluted rain has a slightly acidic pH of 5.6 because carbon dioxide and water in the air react together to form carbonic acid, a weak acid.

365. (A) Acid rain is formed when chemicals react like sulfur dioxide, and nitrogen oxides are released into the air and mix and react with water, oxygen, and other chemicals to form more acidic pollutants, known as acid rain.

366. (C) The pH scale is logarithmic. This means each whole number on the pH scale is 10 times more acidic/more basic than the next value. An example of this would be a pH of 6 is 10 times more acidic than a pH of 7 and 100 times more acidic than a pH of 8.

367. (C) Frogs can tolerate pH levels from 6.5 to 4.

368. (B) An indicator species are species that will be affected the most by small changes in their environment. Clams and snails have the lowest pH range of all of the species in the lake.

369. (D) pH is logarithmic. Each value of 1 is equal to 10 times the next value. So, the difference between 6.5 and 4.5 would be $10 \times 10 = 100\times$ different.

370. (B) When rainwater mixes with carbon dioxide in the atmosphere, carbonic acid is formed.

371. (D) Acid rain affects trees in many ways: damaging the coating on leaves disrupts evaporation and gas exchange, leaching nutrients from soil makes them unavailable to the tree, and toxic metal buildup combined with acid rain stunts growth.

372. (C) Those researching the effects of noise pollution are called bioacoustics researchers. They record sounds using instruments like hydrophones, which record sounds in the ocean.

373. (C) With extended exposure, noises that reach a decibel level of 85 can cause permanent hearing loss.

374. (B) Whale beaching has been associated with noise pollution in the ocean. Whales and other oceanic animals use sonar to communicate with others and their surroundings. Loud sounds can interfere with their ability to navigate and communicate, causing them to get lost or beach themselves.

375. (D) Noise level or loudness is measured in decibels (dB), with high levels over 100 dB causing hearing damage.

Chapter 8: Aquatic and Terrestrial Pollution

376. (A) Smelting ores and burning fossil fuels release sulfur.

377. (B) Burning of fossil fuels releases nitrogen compounds that affect the nitrogen cycle.

378. (C) Municipal water pollution comes from residential and commercial wastewater, which comes from sources such as sewage.

379. (D) Dinoflagellate (or red tide) blooms are caused by storm water runoff and can cause fish and mammal deaths and threaten human health.

380. (C) Water from waste treatment plants is considered a point source because it is released directly into the water supply, whereas the other sources of contamination indirectly lead to the water supply.

381. (B) Phosphorus occurs in low concentrations naturally but is found in high concentrations near populated areas. Excessive phosphate levels lead to eutrophication, in which the oxygen content of water gets depleted. Fish are among the organisms that can die as a result.

382. (C) While radioactive waste is associated with nuclear fission, several industries and products are connected with the production of radioactive waste, including power plants, industry, mining, and medical tracers.

383. (D) Chlorofluorocarbons break down in sunlight, where chlorine-free radicals combine with ozone, breaking it down. They also account for approximately one-quarter of all greenhouse gases that contribute to global warming.

384. (D) Methyl mercury is the by-product that causes health problems.

385. (D) Particulates can cause breathing problems and on a large enough scale can contribute to global warming and ozone depletion.

386. (B) Burning of oil and gas produces all of these chemicals.

387. (D) Nitrate runoff into waterways causes a bloom of algae. These algae will die off, causing a rise in decomposers. These decomposers use up the available oxygen in the water, causing a decrease in available dissolved oxygen for organisms to survive.

388. (D) The Clean Water Act limits the amount (and type) of pollutants that can be discharged in waterways in the United States.

389. (C) Cultural eutrophication is excess nutrients in waterways due to human activity.

390. (D) Secondary sewage treatment is the step in the sewage treatment process that removes any solids through a settling process and uses a biological process to try to remove any organic solids before the water is discharged.

391. (A) Cogeneration recovers otherwise waste heat energy and uses it for heating.

392. (D) Increase in water temperature causes a decrease in the availability of water to hold dissolved oxygen. Therefore, as temperature increases, the amount of dissolved oxygen in the water decreases.

393. (B) Using water as a coolant in power plants is a major cause of thermal pollution. Other causes of thermal pollution include soil erosion.

394. (A) Persistent organic pollutants (POPs) are chemicals that remain unchanged in the environment for very long periods of time. They are often health hazards and can both biomagnify and bioaccumulate in ecosystems.

395. (D) Bald eagles were poisoned with DDT when they ate contaminated fish. Ingested DDT causes the eggshells of the bird offspring to become too soft and brittle.

396. (A) DDT biomagnifies up the food chain. The smallest organisms will collect it into their bodies, and when they are eaten, the toxin moves with them into the larger organism.

397. (D) Toxins magnify as they move up the food chain at approximately (10×) per feeding level.

398. (C) Mercury was in the waste that was dumped into Minamata Bay, Japan, by a chemical company. The mercury then contaminated the fish and other sea creatures living in Minamata Bay. When people ate the fish, mercury poisoned them, and they became ill. Nine hundred people died as a result of this pollution, and 2,265 people suffered from mercury poisoning, now referred to as Minamata disease.

399. (C) The largest predators in a food chain would be most affected by biomagnification.

400. (B) Leachate is produced by water percolating through the waste in a landfill (either through rainfall or through watering of the landfill during compaction).

401. (D) The best way to deal with waste is to reduce it at the source. If we do not create as much waste, we would not have to deal with as much waste.

402. (A) Paper makes up more than 40% of waste in U.S. landfills.

403. (D) Methane is produced during decomposition and is hazardous. Landfills must use collection pipes to make sure that methane doesn't build up in the landfill and cause an explosion or a fire. In addition, methane that is collected can be used to create electricity.

404. (A) The primary stage of sewage water treatment is when the sewage is filtered through sand, allowing particles to settle out.

405. (A) Activated sludge uses aerobic microorganisms that like to digest organic matter that is usually found in sewage.

406. (C) In the United States, ethanol is primarily produced from corn, and if mass ethanol production skyrockets, corn production for fuel could compete with corn production for food, reducing supply and increasing corn prices.

407. (C) LD50 stands for "Lethal Dose" for 50% of the population. LD50 is the dose that would cause the death of 50% (one-half) of a population.

408. (D) The dose-response curve is used to determine the toxicity of a substance. It correlates changes in health with exposure or usage.

409. (C) The LD50 value is where the 50% point intercepts the dose curve.

410. (C) Cholera is a disease caused by drinking water and/or eating food that has been contaminated with a bacterium. Cholera can be a big health issue in third-world countries.

411. (D) Chlorination is used in most large cities because chlorine stays in the water after leaving the treatment plant as opposed to other methods that disinfect at the treatment plant but leave open the possibility that the water gets contaminated again after it leaves.

412. (C) Yucca Mountain is located in Nevada and is a proposed site for long-term storage of high-level radioactive waste from nuclear power generation.

413. (D) Pollution produced by burning garbage subjects communities near waste incinerators to harmful, costly, and avoidable public health risks.

414. (A) Lead poisoning disproportionately affects those in poverty because they tend to live in urban areas where lead was persistent in car exhaust. The lead was then distributed to the soils in the area and has persisted for many years. Also, older houses, which tend to be in more impoverished areas, may have leaded paint that children can be exposed to if they eat it or if it is present in dust or fumes.

(B) Reducing lead emissions from the combustion of fossil fuels in coal power plants, factories, and vehicles can help prevent lead poisoning. Also, by replacing lead pipes, lead can be further eliminated from drinking water. Finally, lead paint can be removed from older homes.

(C) People who live in nonindustrialized countries are still exposed to lead because it is in the atmosphere that was polluted by industrialized countries and therefore contaminates their air and water as well.

415. (A) The LD_{50} is the dose of a chemical at which half of the animals exposed to it die, also known as the lethal dose for 50% of the population. The TD_{50} is the dose of a chemical that is toxic to half of the population, causing some kind of visible negative effect. These measurements are used to determine how toxic a chemical is to a population and whether or not its benefits outweigh its risks.

(B) When the Clean Water Act has no threshold for certain pollutants, it means that no amount of those pollutants is considered acceptable. This assumes that there is no safe level of pollutant that can be tolerated in water. It is simply a zero-tolerance policy.

(C) An ecological gradient near a smokestack that emits SO_2 would show the most loss of plant life where the pollutant concentration is strongest. As the distance from the smokestack increased, the vegetation would be healthier and healthier. The only exception to this rule occurs if the emissions cause acid rain, the area in which pollutants have an effect can be increased.

416. (C) A coliform bacteria test is an indicator of the drinkability of water for human consumption. The test measures the total concentration of coliform bacteria in the water. This bacteria can be associated with water-borne illnesses.

417. (B) Giardiasis is an illness caused by a parasite that lives in the intestines of people and animals. It commonly enters water that has been contaminated by feces.

418. (A) Lyme disease is transmitted to humans through the bite of an infected tick. Lyme disease symptoms can include (but are not limited to) fever, headache, chronic fatigue, and a skin rash.

419. (B) Malaria is caused by a parasite that female mosquitoes transmit when they bite infected people. Female mosquitoes use blood to nurture their eggs.

420. (B) More mosquitoes will cause more mosquito-borne illnesses to spread.

Chapter 9: Global Change

421. (A) The stratospheric ozone layer protects living things from the sun's ultraviolet radiation.

(B) The release of chlorofluorocarbons (CFCs) into the atmosphere causes a problem for molecules of ozone, O_3. Ultraviolet radiation from the sun breaks down CFCs, releasing free chlorine ions that react with O_3 molecules in repeating chain reactions. These reactions can convert O_3 to O_2 and chlorine-oxygen intermediates that continue to react with O_3. This replaces stratospheric O_3 with O_2, which absorbs much less ultraviolet radiation.

(C) The human contribution to ozone in the troposphere comes mostly from burning fossil fuels. In the most common example, nitrogen oxides released by burning fossil fuels create ozone in reactions with volatile organic compounds from automobile exhaust, industrial emissions, chemical solvents, and other sources. Tropospheric ozone can cause many adverse health effects, including a decline in crop yields, lung irritation, asthma, and bronchitis.

422. (B) The ozone layer, residing in the stratosphere, absorbs ultraviolet radiation emitted from the sun.

423. (B) Chlorofluorocarbons (CFCs) are the only greenhouse gases that are solely man-made.

424. (C) Photodissociation is the process by which things break down in sunlight. All three compounds are dangerous when broken down by sunlight because free radicals are formed that then react with ozone, breaking it down.

425. (A) The ozone layer in the earth's stratosphere absorbs UV radiation, and without its protection, there would be more skin cancer, cataracts, and damage to plants and animals.

426. (D) Over 50% of the lower stratospheric ozone is destroyed during the Antarctic spring.

427. (D) The stratospheric ozone layer provides protection from too much ultraviolet radiation from the sun.

428. (C) Energy from ultraviolet light from the sun breaks apart the bonds in an O_2 molecule into a single oxygen atom. The single atom of oxygen is attracted to an O_2 molecule to form an O_3 (ozone) molecule. This molecule of ozone is unstable, so it is constantly being broken apart and reformed in the stratospheric ozone layer.

429. (D) Tradable permits encourage companies to lower emission rates so they can sell the rest of their quota for money.

430. (A) The Montreal Protocol is an international treaty that was signed in order to protect the ozone layer. Its goal it to phase out any production and use of substances (such as CFCs) that destroy the ozone layer.

431. (D) CFCs are any of a class of gases used in refrigerants and aerosol propellants.

432. (B) UV-B: Long-term changes in surface UV-B radiation are important because of potentially harmful effects. There is a relationship between excess UV-B radiation and ozone depletion.

433. (D) The ozone layer can be fully repaired by 2050 if we continue following the recommendations by the Montreal Protocol.

434. (B) The ozone layer is located in the stratosphere. Tropospheric ozone is an air pollutant and is harmful to humans, plants, and animals.

435. (B) Nitrogen oxides come from combustion and are efficient at trapping heat in the atmosphere.

436. (D) Industrialization has led to an increase of about 30% in CO_2 concentration as compared to 250 years ago.

437. (C) About a third of the sunlight reaching earth is reflected back into space, while the rest is absorbed by everything on earth and then gradually goes into the atmosphere.

438. (D) Both deforestation and burning of fossil fuels increase the amount of CO_2 (a greenhouse gas). That increase, as well as the increase in other greenhouse gases, increases the amount of heat radiated back to earth.

439. (D) Some aerosols are made up of chlorofluorocarbons. The other choices are all sources of methane.

440. (C) Warming temperatures both melt the glaciers and cause an expansion of water in the ocean, leading to rising sea levels.

441. (D) El Niño creates warmer ocean temperatures, which contribute heat to the atmosphere.

442. (D) Insects that live in tropical areas and carry disease might benefit from global warming because the size of their potential habitat would increase.

443. (B) Oceans, as well as trees in forests, absorb carbon dioxide, acting as a "sink," or a place to store carbon dioxide.

444. (B) Climate describes the conditions in the atmosphere that are typical for that area for many years. Weather also describes atmospheric conditions but just in the short term.

445. (A) Carbon dioxide levels can be determined by looking at the air bubbles trapped in ice cores, with changes noted at different levels in the core.

446. (B) Polar amplification occurs when the greenhouse effect is amplified by more heat being absorbed by the ocean instead of reflected away by ice, especially in the polar regions.

447. (D) Glacial ice cores preserve samples of atmospheric gases.

448. (A) Methane gas is a greenhouse gas that is produced during anaerobic respiration. The decomposition of organic matter can also contribute to methane gas production.

449. (A) Water vapor is the largest contributor to the earth's greenhouse effect.

450. (A) Water vapor is the most important greenhouse gas. It controls the earth's temperature. On average, it accounts for about 60% of the warming effect.

451. (D) Methane persists on average for about 12 years.

452. (A) China is the largest producer of greenhouse gases in the world as of 2019.

453. (D) CFCs are produced by humans. All of the other choices can be found naturally in the environment.

454. (C) Carbon dioxide is a by-product of the burning of fossil fuels and is considered to be a greenhouse gas.

455. (C) Venus has a toxic, carbon dioxide-rich atmosphere 90 times as thick as earth›s. This large amount of carbon dioxide causes Venus to have a very hot atmosphere.

456. (D) An increase in global temperatures will cause an increase in the evaporation of water, contributing to climate change. This will increase drought conditions in some areas while increasing precipitation and flooding in others.

457. (C) The warming of earth is primarily due to the collection of greenhouse gases in the atmosphere. Scientists have determined that more than 90% of heat from the atmosphere is absorbed by the oceans. As this heat is absorbed by the ocean water, the water expands. Thermal expansion of ocean water is one of the biggest issues of climate change.

458. (B) Ice cores can record climate change from up to 800,000 years ago.

459. (A) Variations in the earth's natural climate cycle, called the Milankovitch cycles. These impact both the seasons and angle of impact of solar energy.

460. (A) El Niño's warmer waters create increased rainfall across the east-central and the eastern Pacific Ocean, especially in the South American west coast. Very wet weather months in April–October can cause major flooding along the coasts of northern Peru and Ecuador

461. (D) In the Northern Hemisphere, there is more land mass than in the Southern Hemisphere. The global carbon dioxide levels increase in the winter due to a lack of photosynthesis in the Northern Hemisphere.

462. (A) Ruminant animals (such as cattle and goats) produce lots of methane gas through belching and flatulence (burps and farts).

463. (D) Wind energy return on energy invested ranges from about 30:1 to about 7:1, with an average of around 18:1. No other alternative energy sources can match that average.

464. (B) Thermal expansion caused by warming of the ocean (since water expands as it warms) is a huge threat to coastal communities all over the world.

465. (A) As ocean water warms up, its ability to hold gases, such as dissolved oxygen, decreases.

466. (D) "Dead zones" occur when there is low or no available dissolved oxygen in the water. This leaves organisms that are unable to flee, suffocate, and die. More mobile species will leave the area, leaving the area barren and lacking life.

467. (B) Fresh and colder water will hold more dissolved gases than water that has dissolved solutes, such as salt and/or warmer waters.

468. (D) Many marine organisms that produce their own shells for shelter, movement, and protection use calcium carbonate as a building material. Decreasing ocean pH has been shown to significantly reduce the availability of calcium carbonate, thus reducing the ability of reef-building corals to produce their skeletons.

469. (D) When carbon dioxide and water are combined, they form a weak acid called carbonic acid.

470. (B) Carbonate ions can help to regulate the pH of seawater.

471. (A) Cold water can dissolve and absorb more carbon dioxide than warm water.

472. (B) pH is referred to as "the power of hydrogen." The higher the H+ concentration, the lower the pH, and the higher the OH− concentration, the higher the pH.

473. (C) The ocean's average pH is now around 8.1, which is considered to be basic, but as the ocean continues to absorb more carbon dioxide, the pH decreases, and the ocean becomes more acidic.

474. (A) Shell-forming animals like corals, crabs, oysters, and urchins are affected most by ocean acidification because it impacts their ability to build their shells.

475. (B) The cane toad of Australia is still considered to be a major pest today. They have no natural predators, can expel a toxin from glands in their skin, and will eat just about anything.

476. (B) Although usually unintentional, invasive species are primarily spread by human activities. A big source of invasive species is cargo ships that can carry aquatic organisms in their ballast water, on their propellers or attached to the bottom of the ship. Small critters such as insects and rodents can get into the wood, shipping palettes, and crates that are shipped around the world.

477. (C) An endemic species is a native species that is found only in a particular area, large or small.

478. (C) Invasive species are alien species that are capable of causing significant harm to our environment, the economy, or society.

479. (D) The lumber company would plan on direct costs, such as the cost of machinery to cut the lumber and the price of fuel to operate the machines. However, other costs, such as loss of tourism dollars and loss of medicinal plants for pharmaceuticals, are known as *externalities*, or *indirect costs*, and are sometimes not taken into consideration by companies when pursuing their business.

480. (C) Even though the United States has only 5% of the world's population, it produces 20% of the world's carbon dioxide emissions.

481. (B) Developing countries use most of their wood for firewood as opposed to developed countries, which use it mostly for construction, paper, and furniture.

482. (D) Restoration always involves attempting to return an area to its previous, unspoiled state—while creating a wetland from ruined grassland can be a good idea, it's not restoration.

483. (B) Costa Rica is the world leader in protecting the greatest proportion of its biodiversity.

484. (B) The Marine Mammal Protection Act (1972) forbids the killing of any marine mammals or selling of their body parts for profit or research.

485. (B) Species that have specialized feeding habits find it harder to find food if their environment changes.

486. (D) When two populations join, they can trade genes widely, dispersing more traits among the whole enlarged group.

487. (B) The bushmeat trade in Africa is a big problem because people are illegally hunting endangered species as a source of income and selling it in black markets.

488. (B) Bushmeat can be a source of Ebola because infections have been associated with hunting, butchering, and processing meat from infected animals.

489. (C) Rainforests are the most biologically diverse biomes on the planet.

490. (A) One of the risks of having a large area to maintain biodiversity is that a natural disaster could devastate an ecosystem.

491. (C) A habitat corridor is an area of habitat that is untouched by humans that connects wildlife populations that would otherwise be separated by human structures (such as roads or homes).

492. (A) Habitat fragmentation describes the breaking apart of an organism's preferred habitat, causing populations to be separated (fragmented). This process causes a decrease in biodiversity.

493. (C) The pharmaceutical industry estimates that $30 billion comes from biodiversity annually.

494. (B) The bottleneck effect is defined by a drastic reduction in the size of a population due to something like a natural disaster.

495. (D) It is estimated that 99% of all species on the planet are now extinct.

496. (A) A field of corn would have a lot of one species (high species abundance) but a low species diversity (only one thing).

497. (C) One of the major contributors to a decrease in biodiversity is poaching of species to extinction.

498. (D) Overfishing is a problem associated with fishing too many of the same species and driving that species to extinction.

499. (B) Papahānaumokuākea Marine National Monument contains about 583,000 square miles of ocean waters. It is one of the world's largest protected areas and the largest in the United States.

500. (A) Artificial selection is the process where humans select traits that are considered to be desirable, such as larger crops or juicier fruit, and they breed them specifically to obtain the best results possible.